Survive and Thrive as a Physical Educator

STRATEGIES FOR THE FIRST YEAR AND BEYOND

ALISA R. JAMES

Human Kinetics

Library of Congress Cataloging-in-Publication Data

James, Alisa R.
  Survive and thrive as a physical educator : strategies for the first year and beyond / Alisa R. James.
      p. cm.
  Includes bibliographical references and index.
  ISBN 978-1-4504-1199-8 (soft cover) -- ISBN 1-4504-1199-1 (soft cover) 1. Physical education and training--Study and teaching--United States. 2. Physical education teachers--Training of--United States. 3. First year teachers. I. Title.
  GV362.J35 2012
  613.707--dc23
                                    2012011058

ISBN-10: 1-4504-1199-1 (print)
ISBN-13: 978-1-4504-1199-8 (print)

Acquisitions Editor: Cheri Scott; **Developmental Editor:** Ray Vallese; **Assistant Editor:** Derek Campbell; **Copyeditor:** Patrick Connolly; **Indexer:** Michael Ferreira; **Graphic Designers:** Bob Reuther and Joe Buck; **Graphic Artist:** Denise Lowry; **Cover Designers:** Bob Reuther and Keith Blomberg; **Photographer (cover):** © Human Kinetics; **Photographer (interior):** © Human Kinetics, unless otherwise noted; photos on pp. 44, 100, 103, and 213 © Alisa R. James; **Photo Asset Manager:** Laura Fitch; **Photo Production Manager:** Jason Allen; **Art Manager:** Kelly Hendren; **Associate Art Manager:** Alan L. Wilborn; **Illustrations:** © Human Kinetics; **Printer:** United Graphics

Printed in the United States of America   10 9 8 7 6 5 4 3 2 1

The paper in this book is certified under a sustainable forestry program.

Human Kinetics
Website: www.HumanKinetics.com

United States: Human Kinetics, P.O. Box 5076, Champaign, IL 61825-5076
800-747-4457
e-mail: humank@hkusa.com

Canada: Human Kinetics, 475 Devonshire Road Unit 100, Windsor, ON N8Y 2L5
800-465-7301 (in Canada only)
e-mail: info@hkcanada.com

Europe: Human Kinetics, 107 Bradford Road
Stanningley, Leeds LS28 6AT, United Kingdom
+44 (0) 113 255 5665
e-mail: hk@hkeurope.com

Australia: Human Kinetics, 57A Price Avenue, Lower Mitcham, South Australia 5062
08 8372 0999
e-mail: info@hkaustralia.com

New Zealand: Human Kinetics, P.O. Box 80, Torrens Park, South Australia 5062
0800 222 062
e-mail: info@hknewzealand.com

E5484

To my family, for their support and belief in me.

Contents

Preface

Welcome to the gymnasium and to the profession of physical educator. For years you have been in the role of a student, working to complete assignments, working with professors and in-service teachers, and learning what it takes to be a skillful physical education teacher. Now, as you enter the gymnasium as the teacher, you will design and deliver those assignments, work with diverse students and teachers, and continue your education as a professional.

If you are like most beginning teachers, you are experiencing both excitement and fear. You have a good idea of what you and your students are supposed to do; however, you are unsure of how successful you will be as a teacher. For example, how will you handle discipline issues? How will you motivate students? Will the students cooperate with you and engage in your planned learning tasks?

There is no reason to fear. Everyone has these questions—and many other questions—when they begin a teaching career. Teaching physical education is hard work. On a given day, you may find that one class is engaged in the lesson and is excited to participate, while the same lesson fails miserably in the next class. Even veteran teachers experience days when they are frustrated and do not know what to do—and other days when they are able to motivate students to learn and participate in physical education.

Your initial years of teaching physical education can be extremely challenging. You might feel overwhelmed by the daily pressures of planning and assessing, dealing with behavior issues, and meeting the individual needs of your students. These pressures can be exhausting and may at times leave you questioning if you really want to be a teacher.

As an associate professor in a large PETE (physical education teacher education) program at a comprehensive college, I have clearly seen that student teachers and new teachers need support and advice in order to become skilled physical education teachers. New teachers face several challenges, including limited support from the university as well as minimal supervision and mentoring.

The purpose of *Survive and Thrive as a Physical Educator: Strategies for the First Year and Beyond* is twofold. First, the book serves as a resource that helps beginning teachers successfully transfer what they learned in college to the setting in which they teach physical education. Second, the book provides information and useful resources that beginning teachers did not learn about as part of their undergraduate preparation; this information is essential in helping teachers succeed as physical educators.

The book is divided into two parts. Part I, composed of five chapters, is dedicated to helping beginning teachers take what they learned in college and transfer it to their teaching setting. Chapter 1 discusses strategies that will help you fit in and become an active and contributing member of the school community. Chapter 2 contains ideas for the beginning of the school year, from organizing the gymnasium to setting goals for the first week of school. Chapter 3 focuses on the task of creating lesson and unit plans. It provides you with guidelines for planning effective lessons and units, as well as ideas for delivering effective instruction for all students. Chapter 4 describes how to assess and evaluate student progress, and it addresses grading in physical education. Chapter 5 focuses on classroom and behavior management, which is a major concern for beginning teachers. The chapter describes the process of establishing the learning environment as well as developing rules, routines, and expectations. In addition, it discusses techniques for promoting good behavior along with consequences that may be used to address misbehavior.

Part II of the book focuses on things that beginning teachers may not have learned in college but are nevertheless crucial to their success in teaching physical education. Chapter 6 covers methods that can be used to motivate students in physical education. Various types of motivation are discussed as well as specific strategies for motivating students in physical education. Chapter 7 explores diversity in the physical education classroom and how this diversity affects physical education. Chapter 8 illustrates the importance of understanding how schools socialize beginning teachers, and it presents strategies for dealing with the effects of socialization. In addition, the chapter discusses teacher burnout and what you can do to alleviate the effects of burnout. Chapter 9 offers suggestions for developing relationships with parents and guardians, and it describes how to communicate with them in a positive manner. Chapter 10 focuses on the importance of professional development and how it can help you become an effective teacher.

Each chapter contains several useful resources, including templates ranging from sample assessments to sample letters that can be sent home to parents. Note that while the templates included in the book can be photocopied, I encourage you to modify them to fit your specific teaching situation or to create your own. You will find the following resources grouped at the end of their respective chapters.

In addition, each chapter has questions that will help you reflect on the content in regard to your teaching practice.

The book also includes two appendixes that are beneficial for beginning teachers. Appendix A provides answers to frequently asked questions ranging from how to prepare for a substitute teacher to questions about the tenure process. Appendix B identifies a variety of resources, including print and electronic resources as well as equipment suppliers.

This book was written to serve as a guide to help new teachers not only survive but also thrive as physical education teachers. I hope that you find the book informative and useful in helping you to become a skillful physical educator who continues to be passionate about teaching.

PART I

Skills to Help You Survive

CHAPTER 1

Your First Job as a Physical Educator— Now What?

A beginning physical education teacher will encounter many challenges. One of your first challenges is to avoid being overwhelmed by the numerous responsibilities that come with the profession. In addition to the tasks that come with the job, you will likely face additional stress related to the transition from student to professional. Fortunately, by taking some specific steps, you can make this transition easier and be on your way to becoming a successful physical educator. This chapter discusses those steps and covers issues such as learning about the school district and community, becoming familiar with policies and procedures, and developing relationships with your colleagues in the school.

School District, School, and Community

The first step is to learn as much as you can about the school district, the school, and the community in which you will be teaching.

First, you need to become acquainted with your school district and the school in which you will be working. Visit your assigned school and spend time exploring its layout. Examine the facilities and equipment that are available for physical education. Some schools have excellent facilities for teaching as well as an abundance of equipment; however, that might not be the case in the school where you are teaching. Some schools do not have any outdoor space, while others may not have enough equipment for you to teach in a manner that maximizes participation. In my first teaching assignment, I taught in a space that was not only the gym but also the cafeteria. It was a decently sized space, but the floor was tiled, and the cafeteria tables were folded into the wall; the tables were precariously held in place by wire, which gave me pause each time a child got close or a ball hit a table. The point is that you should know the space and equipment available to you for teaching and should plan your program accordingly.

The Internet is a helpful tool for gaining information about your school and the school district. Be sure to investigate the school district's website as well as the website for your particular school. While examining the websites, look specifically for web pages dedicated to physical education. Significant information regarding the curriculum and policies for physical education can often be found on these pages.

In addition to learning about the school and the district, you should spend time in the community to get a feel for the people who live there. Make an effort to learn about the points of pride, recreational activities, businesses, and opportunities for physical activity that exist in the community. Another way to gain an understanding of the community is to visit websites that give information about the area. A great website for finding information about any community in the United States is www.epodunk.com. The website provides valuable information such as median income of residents, educational level of residents, school enrollment, and parks and recreational opportunities in the community. As you research the school and the community, try to gain information about the ethnic and cultural backgrounds and values of students and their parents. Also try to determine the socioeconomic status of the students' families. Resource 1.1 is a questionnaire that will help you assess important aspects of the community in which you teach. Resource 1.2 enables you to identify physical activity opportunities in the community.

Policies and Procedures

Once you have become familiar with your school, school district, and community, the next step is to examine the policies and procedures of the district and school. At the start of the year, you will be barraged with a lot of information regarding policies and procedures, and you will be expected to learn this information in a short period of time. District policies are policies that apply to all teachers, staff, and students in the district. School policies apply to the teachers, staff, and students in a particular school. Most school districts provide new teachers with an employee handbook that explains the policies and procedures for the school and district in detail.

You need to understand district- and schoolwide policies and procedures because they affect your school life and your success as a teacher. For example, make sure you understand the district policies concerning physical education curriculum, district grading procedures, tenure policies, staff evaluation policies and procedures, emergency school closing procedures, and reporting periods for grades and progress reports. You must seek clarification of policies and procedures that you do not understand; otherwise, you risk making mistakes that could have an impact on your effectiveness as a teacher or your chances of being evaluated in a favorable manner. Here are several types of policies and procedures that you need to know:

- ▶ Policies concerning teacher arrival and dismissal times
- ▶ Policies regarding expected dress for teachers
- ▶ Code of discipline for students
- ▶ Policies for acceptable student behavior
- ▶ Consequences for inappropriate student behavior
- ▶ Lesson plan format and review procedures

- ▶ Teacher duties and responsibilities (recess, bus, and so on)
- ▶ Student attendance procedures
- ▶ How to call for a substitute
- ▶ How to handle student injuries
- ▶ Emergency procedures (fire, tornado, school intruder)

Professional Relationships

When you are trying to learn the policies and procedures at your school, one valuable source of information is your professional colleagues. Set aside time to get to know your colleagues and develop professional relationships with them. Your colleagues include teaching faculty, school administrators, and support staff. They are valuable resources and will be instrumental in helping you through the first few years of teaching. Try to meet your colleagues and spend time getting to know them by asking questions and seeking advice about effective teaching.

Teaching Faculty

Developing professional relationships with other teachers in your building is vital to your success as a beginning teacher. All teachers, not only physical education teachers, can help you understand the school as a workplace and can provide valuable information regarding students, parents, administrators, and the community at large.

In my own experience as a beginning teacher, many teaching colleagues had an influence on my success as a teacher; however, one teacher in particular helped me understand my students and their families. This teacher also helped me understand the influence that the community and certain students' home situations had on the performance and behavior of the students. Mrs. Jones was a music teacher at my school and was a very successful teacher. The students respected and trusted her. The countless hours I spent in conversations with her and observing her interactions with students had a great impact on my teaching style and how I interacted with students.

Administrators

The administrators in your building will typically be principals or assistant principals. These administrators are the instructional leaders of the school, and they can help you with a variety of concerns related to instruction, classroom management, and professional development. At the beginning of the school year, one important task for you to undertake is to meet with the school principal. In this meeting, you should

▶ Ask questions of other teachers to learn more about your school's policies and procedures.

confirm your teaching schedule and other school responsibilities—such as homeroom, study hall, bus, lunch, recess duty, and safety patrol.

During this meeting, you should ask about the school's expectations and norms. Some of these expectations and norms will be explained in the teacher handbook; however, you must be sure to ask questions about any expectations that are not clear. In addition, ask about the principal's perspectives on the successful delivery of instruction. Also try to find out the principal's beliefs about the role that physical education plays in the overall education of students. Don't be intimidated about meeting with the principal at the beginning of the year. Although administrators are often short on time and overwhelmed with a variety of tasks, their responsibilities include guiding and assisting new teachers in the school.

The director of physical education is an administrator who may not be located in your building; however, you should meet with this administrator to discuss his or her expectations of physical education teachers. You can also clarify any questions you may have about the district's physical education curriculum or instructional and assessment practices. If the director of physical education is not located in your building, you should make an appointment to meet with this person outside of the school day. Discuss your vision of physical education as well as any questions or concerns you may have. In addition, you can ask the director to come observe you teaching and to offer feedback regarding your teaching performance. The following are questions that a beginning teacher may want to ask an administrator.

- ▶ How do I get keys to the gym and equipment room?
- ▶ Will I have paraeducators who will help me in physical education? What are the responsibilities of the paraeducators and how are they trained? (Paraeducators are professionals who assist the physical education teacher or the special education teacher in the classroom. Chapter 7 provides more information about working with paraeducators.)
- ▶ How do I get assistance from the office for emergencies or discipline problems?
- ▶ How do I make a discipline referral?
- ▶ What is the teaching schedule?
- ▶ Will I be assigned a mentor teacher?
- ▶ How will I be evaluated?
- ▶ How often will I be evaluated?
- ▶ What are my other duties?

▶ Meeting with administrators can help to clarify what is expected of you as a new physical education teacher.

Support Staff

Support staff members—such as secretaries, custodians, and nurses—are important to schools because they have a direct impact on the school climate and environment. Support staff members are often the first individuals whom visitors encounter on entering the school. One of the best things you can do is to develop professional relationships with support staff and to seek ways to help them. The assistance that these staff members provide to you is crucial to your success.

School secretaries are important partners and can be a great resource for you. They possess a great deal of knowledge regarding how the school and district function. They can provide essential information such as clarification of school policies; how to obtain keys for the gymnasium, office, and equipment rooms; and how to order equipment.

School custodians are also very important colleagues for a physical education teacher. You will need assistance from the custodial staff in many situations. For example, you may need the custodian to help when the gym floor is wet, to clean the floor after a child gets sick, or to change the lights in the gymnasium. You should establish a positive relationship with the custodial staff and help them whenever possible. Furthermore, you should ask them how they would like you to handle situations such as spills in the gymnasium, needed repairs to physical education facilities, and problems with outdoor spaces used for physical education.

The school nurse is another important colleague. The nurse can provide you with students' health histories and can offer advice concerning students' medical conditions. In addition, the nurse can provide you with supplies for a first aid kit to be kept in the gymnasium. The nurse can also help you develop procedures to be followed in case of a student injury.

As part of getting to know your colleagues, you should observe the interactions between them. By watching these interactions, you can get a feel for the social system that operates within the school. The social system that operates in a school consists of colleagues' behaviors and how they communicate and work with each other. Interactions between colleagues are often influenced by their values and backgrounds, and differences in these factors can sometimes create tension between colleagues. You should attempt to understand colleagues' values and backgrounds because these factors may influence your interactions with those colleagues.

Understanding the intricacies of your colleagues' interactions and learning to work well with your colleagues will take time and patience. Here are some specific actions you can take to fit in and become an accepted member of the school community:

1. Learn your colleagues' names and always say good morning and good evening to them.
2. Use good manners and offer to help others in any way that you can.

3. Speak positively about students and be friendly to everyone in an effort to avoid cliques.

4. Be on time for duty assignments such as bus duty or recess duty.

5. Make it a point to meet with your physical education colleagues. You may have physical education colleagues in your building; however, you may not. You should try to meet the physical education colleagues in your building as well as those in other buildings. At the beginning of the year, school districts often have meetings that give you the opportunity to meet physical education colleagues who work at other schools in the district. Be sure to introduce yourself and begin to develop professional relationships with these individuals. You can also ask them if you may contact them with questions that may arise, or you can even ask for the opportunity to come and watch them teach.

6. Strive to be the best physical education teacher in your building, district, and state. Your efforts to be a great teacher will be noticed, and you will be a valued member in your school district.

Summary

You can do several things to prepare yourself for the transition from student to professional physical education teacher. First, visit the school and examine the facilities and equipment. Second, use the Internet to gain information about the school, the school district, and the community. Third, get to know your teaching colleagues and the support staff, and take steps to interact with them in a positive manner. Fourth, review the employee handbook to gain an understanding of district- and schoolwide policies and procedures. Finally, meet with your building principal and the director of physical education to discuss questions you may have as well as your goals as a teacher. Engaging in these actions will enable you to get a great start as a beginning physical education teacher.

DISCUSSION QUESTIONS

1. Why is it important for beginning teachers to learn about the school, the school district, and the community in which they teach?

2. What things would you do in order to learn about the school, the school district, and the community?

3. What actions would you take to build relationships with administrators, teaching colleagues, and support staff?

Assessment of Community Members

1. What do people in the community do for physical activity?

_____

_____

2. Does the community have public transportation?

_____

_____

3. Does the school district have support in the community?

_____

_____

4. What type of dwelling do most of your students live in (single-family houses, apartment buildings, and so on)?

_____

_____

5. Do most residents own or rent?

_____

_____

6. Are most of the households headed by two parents?

_____

_____

7. What is the average level of education of the members of the community?

_____

_____

(continued)

8. What businesses are located in the community?

_____

_____

9. What kind of jobs do residents hold?

_____

_____

10. What is the average socioeconomic level of members of the community?

_____

_____

11. What are the racial and ethnic backgrounds of community members?

_____

_____

12. What are the values of community members?

_____

_____

13. What are community members proud of?

_____

_____

14. What do community members hope for?

_____

_____

15. What do community members disapprove of?

_____

_____

From A. James, 2013, *Survive and thrive as a physical educator: Strategies for the first year and beyond* (Champaign, IL: Human Kinetics).

Checklist for Physical Activity Resources in the Community

Community resource for physical activity	Present in community	Absent in community
Bicycle paths		
Bowling lanes		
Golf course		
Dance studio		
Frisbee golf course		
Golf driving range		
Handball or racquetball courts		
Hiking trails		
Horseback riding stables		
Lake area (fishing or boating)		
Orienteering course		
Ice rink		
Roller rink		
Downhill slopes (ski or snowboard)		
Swimming pool		
Tennis courts		
Fitness center		
Parks		
Basketball courts		
Other		

From A. James, 2013, *Survive and thrive as a physical educator: Strategies for the first year and beyond* (Champaign, IL: Human Kinetics).

CHAPTER 2

Ready, Set, Go! Starting the School Year Right

M any teachers—even those with experience—feel overwhelmed at the beginning of the school year because there is a lot to do in a very short period of time. As a beginning teacher, you should remember that you have some advantages over your experienced colleagues. For example, you have received cutting-edge training as part of your undergraduate education. You have been exposed to state-of-the-art instructional and assessment techniques that some of your colleagues may not be aware of (because they haven't been in a college classroom or pursued professional development opportunities recently). A second advantage is your enthusiasm for teaching. You have spent several years studying and practicing how to teach, and now you are ready to implement your knowledge and show your enthusiasm within your own classroom.

Being a recently certified teacher may give you some advantages over your colleagues, but you will also encounter several problems as a result of your lack of experience. For example, you may become frustrated with the curriculum, or you may find that equipment and facilities are lacking. Moreover, you may have difficulty balancing teaching and coaching duties. In addition, you may not know how to respond to students in situations that require discipline. One way to minimize problems caused by your lack of experience is to take steps to prepare for the school year in advance.

This chapter focuses on helping you get the school year off to a good start. It covers tasks that need to be completed before the beginning of the school year as well as on the first day of school. Furthermore, the chapter discusses the importance of managing your time and the paperwork associated with being a teacher.

Managing Time and Paperwork

Beginning teachers have to learn to juggle many responsibilities, both instructional and noninstructional. You need to develop time management skills as well as a system for managing and organizing paperwork in order to eliminate missed meetings and deadlines.

To help manage your time effectively, you can do several things. One is to create a daily schedule to ensure that tasks are accomplished. You can also use a date planner or the calendar on your cell phone to record all scheduled staff meetings, coaching responsibilities, and meetings with colleagues and parents. Finally, you need to organize teaching materials and correspondence. One way to do this is to use binders to file correspondence such as e-mails, memos, letters, parent phone call logs, discipline logs, and any other pertinent materials. Binders can also be used to organize unit and lesson plans. In addition, computers or tablets such as the iPad can be used to create and store the latter documents in electronic files.

In addition to developing a system for organizing paperwork, you should develop a personal employment file containing paperwork that relates to your position as a physical education teacher. An employment file is important for several reasons. First, the file ensures that important documents are easily accessible when they are needed. Second, the file is a great place to store documentation of professional development activities; you will need to submit this documentation to your human resource department in order to keep your certification current. Finally, if at some point you decide to seek employment in another district, this file will ensure that you have the information necessary to apply for different positions. The contents of this folder should include a copy of your contract, school and district rosters (including phone numbers and e-mail addresses), benefit forms, copies of professional membership cards, documentation of professional development activities, district calendars, the employee handbook, your current resume, and a copy of your teaching certification.

This folder should be updated throughout the year and at the beginning of each school year. In addition, the folder should be kept in a secure place that is easily accessible. Resource 2.1 is a checklist for the personal employment folder. Resource 2.2 is a template for a school and district roster that includes phone numbers and e-mail addresses.

One Month Before School Begins

You should begin getting ready for the school year about one month in advance of the start of the year. One month will provide ample time for you to complete the tasks that will enable you to begin the school year effectively. One of the first things you should do is learn your daily schedule and post it in your office. In addition, you should inspect the equipment and facilities that are available for physical education, taking an inventory of the equipment. Resource 2.3 is a sample form that can be used to record your equipment inventory.

Facilities and field spaces that are used for instruction should also be inspected. Inspect the gymnasium floor for areas in disrepair, and ensure that the lighting is adequate and that lights are secured to the ceiling. In addition, make sure that the walls of the gymnasium do not have anything protruding from them that a student can run into. Crash mats should cover the walls.

Indoor and outdoor spaces for teaching physical education vary greatly. Some schools may have ample indoor and outdoor space; however, other schools may have minimal facilities and may even lack outdoor space. Fields that are used for physical education should also be inspected. Fields should be free of debris and free of divots or holes that students may step into and injure themselves. Resource 2.4 is a tool you can use when inspecting indoor and outdoor facilities. Make sure you follow the proper procedures to have any necessary repairs done to equipment or facilities before the beginning of the school year.

Next, you should review the district's physical education curriculum guide. The curriculum guide should be provided at the time of hire. If not, make sure you ask for a copy. The curriculum guide provides a framework of the content that you are expected to teach at your school. You should ask questions about any aspect of the curriculum guide that is not clear. After reviewing the curriculum guide, you should develop a

▶ One month before school begins, test equipment to be sure it is in good working order.

full-year plan for each grade level that you will be teaching. For example, if you are teaching in an elementary school that has grades three to five, the curriculum plan would include all the content units that you will teach at each of those grade levels. Creating a full-year plan will be discussed in detail in chapter 3. The curriculum plan should be kept in a plan book so that it is easily accessible when you are creating unit plans.

After creating full-year plans for each grade level that you will teach, you can begin planning the first units of instruction that will be presented to students. If time permits, you may want to plan the first two units before the beginning of school. This preplanning is beneficial because paperwork and other duties that you will need to perform at the beginning of the school year could interfere with your ability to plan the units during the first weeks of school.

Finally, a month before the school year begins, you should create a set of professional goals to help motivate you throughout the school year. Professional goals are important because they serve as a map of where you would like to go as a professional. For example, a professional goal may be that you would like to do a presentation at a conference or serve on the school wellness committee. Whatever your professional goals, you need to create an action plan to reach those goals. In this action plan, you identify specific steps you will take to reach your goals and record your progress toward meeting those goals. Setting professional development goals and developing a plan for reaching these goals are discussed further in chapter 10. Be sure to place a copy of these goals in your employment folder (which was discussed earlier in the chapter). This will make it easy to examine the goals along with the documentation of your professional development activities in order to evaluate the degree to which you have met your goals.

The following list presents other tasks that need to be completed a month before school begins. Perhaps one of the most important tasks is to decide on classroom rules, routines, and expectations. This will be discussed in detail in chapter 5.

▶ Create visual aids such as signs, posters, bulletin boards, and so on.

▶ Create a sign with rules to be posted in the gymnasium.

▶ Inspect your teaching wardrobe to ensure that it is appropriate for a professional physical education teacher.

▶ Enter scheduled events from the school calendar into a personal planner.

▶ Join your professional organizations—both at the national (American Alliance for Health, Physical Education, Recreation and Dance) and at the state level.

▶ Check with the school nurse about any student health concerns.

▶ Review students' individualized education plans (IEPs) and speak with teachers and aides about any concerns or questions. Plan how to provide modifications to lessons for students with IEPs.

Two Weeks Before School Begins

Two weeks before the school year begins, you should be setting up your office and desk. The organization of the office is very important. You will want to secure several supplies. Typically, supplies will be stored in a storage room or the main office. Ask the school secretary how to obtain supplies and how to order any needed supplies that are not available. Some important supplies that you'll need include a planning book for planning lessons, a grade book, and an attendance book.

During this time, you should create a library of resources that will be kept in your office. Your library should include methods textbooks, activity notebooks, books describing various assessment techniques and curriculum models, and books that contain information about how to perform and teach various activities.

You can use several methods to find resources for your professional library. First, you can use a search engine such as Google to search the web for physical education titles. Second, you can go to websites such as Amazon.com and Abebooks.com to search for resources. Finally, several publishers such as Human Kinetics (humankinetics.com) specialize in physical education and physical activity titles.

Another useful resource to have in your library is professional journals. Professional journals provide cutting-edge information regarding physical education, as well as thought-provoking articles that further your professional development as a teacher. Two of the most commonly read professional journals are *The Journal of Physical Education, Recreation and Dance* and *Strategies,* which are published by the American Alliance for Health, Physical Education, Recreation and Dance (AAHPERD) and are available with membership to the AAHPERD. AAHPERD is the national professional organization for physical education and will be discussed in more detail in chapter 10.

One Week Before School Begins

One week before the school year begins, you need to get the gym ready for students by posting the rules and any other signs, bulletin boards, or visual aids on the wall. Make sure that the signs hung on the wall are neat and professional. As a teacher, I went to a professional sign shop and had them create vinyl signs listing my rules and expectations. These signs were durable and economical. Furthermore, I was able to attach Velcro to the back of the signs, which allowed me to put them up and remove them daily.

Several organizations such as the American Heart Association and AAHPERD have posters available that can be used on bulletin boards or hung on the walls. Be sure to laminate any posters in order to preserve them. Avoid leaving posters and signs on the wall that are torn and tattered, because doing so conveys the message that their content is not important. Teachers should also create an emergency plan to be posted on the wall. This emergency plan should include provisions for how to deal with medical emergencies, fire, tornado, earthquakes, and situations when the school may go into lockdown because students might be in danger during the school day. School districts mandate plans for dealing with these emergencies, and you need to understand and follow these procedures during an emergency.

During this time, you will also want to place your class rosters into a grade book and a computer spreadsheet program. Study the names on the class roster and make sure that you can pronounce them correctly. Also, a week before the school year begins, you should review lesson plans for the first unit of instruction (as discussed previously, these lessons should be planned a month before the school year is scheduled to begin).

In addition, you need to create a substitute teacher folder in case you must be absent from your job. This folder should include your contact information, daily schedule, class rosters, attendance forms, rules and routines, explanation of daily duties, instructions on how to access keys to the office and equipment room, discipline plan, a list of reliable students, emergency procedures, and lesson plans that are easy to implement. It is also helpful to include a feedback form with specific questions that will allow the substitute to provide you with information regarding instruction and student behavior. Resource 2.5 is a sample feedback form that could be part of a substitute folder. Moreover, you should leave the name and room number of a trusted colleague whom the substitute can turn to for help during the day if necessary. A copy of the substitute folder should be kept in the main office so that the substitute will receive the folder when reporting to the office for the day.

A crucial task to be completed a week before the school year begins is to create a beginning-of-school welcome letter that explains classroom rules, expectations, grading policies, policies in regard to dress, and so on. This letter helps set the tone for the school year both with parents and with students. Include a section of the letter that must be signed and returned to the teacher; this will provide documentation that parents are aware of the rules and procedures that exist in physical education. A sample letter is provided in chapter 9. This letter should be sent to parents on the first day of school. Students commonly bring home several forms for their parents to sign and return with their child at the beginning of the school year.

Finally, you need to set first-week goals. Make it a goal to learn students' names and get to know students. Getting to know the students will take time, but several avenues are available for gaining information about students. One way is to review students' records; however, you must be sure to follow confidentiality procedures that may be in place in your district. Another strategy is to speak with guidance counselors or other teachers. Keep an open mind when speaking with these individuals and remain fairly objective so you do not bias your opinion of a particular student based on their comments.

The best way to get to know students is to ask them questions. For example, give students a worksheet that asks them questions about what they like to do outside of school, about their family, and so on. Resource 2.6 provides an example of this type of questionnaire. If you like, you can create a form that shares personal information about you

▶ One way to get to know students is to have them fill out a worksheet with information about themselves. You can fill one out as well.

with your students. Make sure you only share appropriate information as well as information that you are comfortable sharing. For example, you may want to share information regarding your favorite sports and activities or information regarding your family or pets. When interacting with students, express an interest in them as they reveal information about themselves and their lives. You can also attend school and community events that students attend in order to have another venue for connecting with students.

One day before school begins, you should finish any tasks that have not yet been completed. In addition, you may want to reread the material in your faculty handbook and ask any last-minute questions, as well as review students' medical concerns with the school nurse. Finally, you should organize any equipment or paperwork that is needed for the first day of school.

First Day of School

Now that you have prepared your teaching station (i.e., gymnasium, multipurpose room, and so on), reviewed your lesson plans, and tied up loose ends, it is time to give some thought to the first day of school. Being nervous about the first day is normal; however, your students will also be anxious as well as excited. The first day is very important because it will set the tone for the entire school year.

The first thing you need to think about is professionalism. A professional physical education teacher demonstrates several professional behaviors. Behaviors such as dressing professionally, being punctual, and being enthusiastic are all significant. On the first day of school, you must dress professionally and make sure that you are well groomed. Appropriate dress for a physical education teacher includes wearing collared polo shirts or performance style shirts that have appropriate logos. Shirts should be long enough to be tucked in and cover the lower back. Pants should be professional athletic pants that are appropriate in cut and style. Shorts should be a suitable length so they are not too short. Clothes should be clean and free of wrinkles. Dressing in this manner demonstrates a high level of self-confidence and respect. Enthusiasm is another professional behavior that you need to demonstrate daily, but it is of the utmost importance on the first day of school. Students enjoy physical education or any other subject when their teachers demonstrate enthusiasm for what they are teaching.

Your enthusiasm and training will help you meet your professional responsibilities as a physical education teacher. You must have a good understanding of your responsibilities because this knowledge will help you get the year off to a good start—and help you be successful

▶ On the first day of school, it is especially important to dress professionally and show enthusiasm for class activities.

throughout the year. The following list discusses some professional responsibilities that will help you start the school year successfully.

- ▶ **Be prepared for class.** Plan instruction for learning and know your subject matter. Develop content that is interesting and sequential. Set aside enough time to plan and gather resources to help cover weak content areas. Create libraries of both electronic and print resources that will be useful when planning units of instruction.

- ▶ **Teach and assess for learning.** Focus on learning outcomes. Assess students to ensure that they achieve the learning outcomes and become physically educated individuals.

- ▶ **Set professional goals.** Setting professional goals will improve your teaching skills and give you something to work toward.

- ▶ **Dress the part of a professional physical education teacher.** If you look like a professional physical educator, people will treat you as a professional.

- ▶ **Create an inviting atmosphere in the gymnasium.** Make your gym attractive by using posters and bulletin boards. Get to know your students and make them feel capable.
- ▶ **Maintain order in the gymnasium.** Establish rules and routines, and take charge of your class.
- ▶ **Be optimistic and enthusiastic.** Each day will have challenges; however, you must be enthusiastic and look at challenges as opportunities, not setbacks.
- ▶ **Seek support from colleagues.** All teachers can benefit from the experiences of their colleagues. Colleagues can offer solutions, support, and encouragement to help you succeed.
- ▶ **Be committed to professionalism.** Be professional in all aspects of your profession, from interacting with students, colleagues, and parents to being a leader in your school. Become a member of your state and national AHPERD in order to stay abreast of advocacy issues and professional development opportunities in physical education.

On the first day of school, you should confidently meet the students at the door of the gymnasium and introduce yourself. At the elementary level, you may want to wear a name tag to help students remember your name. Next, you should teach students your rules, routines, and expectations. There are several ways to do this. One way is to stand in front of your students and explain these things; however, depending on the developmental level of students, you can use a variety of exciting techniques that will engage students as they learn the rules and expectations.

For instance, you can hand out index cards and ask the students to write down what they believe the classroom rules and expectations should be. Afterward, have students get into small groups and decide on the rule and expectation that they believe are most important. Have each group present their rule and expectation to the class along with a rationale regarding the importance of the rule and expectation. Finally, have the class choose one rule and expectation that will be in effect for their class in addition to the rules and expectations that are in effect for all classes.

As another example, you could create a short video that features you teaching the rules, routines, and expectations. This video could be in the form of a public service announcement, music video, or you reporting from a remote location such as New York City. The video could be viewed in class or in a media center where each student views the video on a computer. After students view the recording, give them a short written assessment regarding your rules, routines, and expectations.

Next, you will teach your lesson. You should teach the first lesson as if it was the most important lesson of the year because you want students to be excited about coming to physical education every day. Throughout the lesson, focus on teaching and reinforcing routines such as start and stop signals, home base, drink and bathroom breaks, and so on. At the end of class, remind students of the routine for leaving the gymnasium. Finally, thank students for a great first day and let them know that you look forward to the next class meeting.

Summary

Getting the school year off to a good start is of utmost importance to a beginning teacher. You need to do several things in order to be prepared for the new school year. You must develop a time management system that allows you to create daily schedules and keep track of important meetings. In addition, you need to create a system for managing paperwork, including correspondence from administrators, colleagues, and parents. Creating a professional employment folder enables you to store documents related to your teaching career, such as your teaching certification, professional membership cards, teaching contract, professional goals, and documentation of professional development activities.

One month before the school year begins, you need to undertake several tasks. These tasks include learning your daily schedule; creating an equipment inventory; inspecting facilities and equipment; reviewing the curriculum guide; and finalizing rules, routines, and expectations for your classes. In addition, you should set up your office and create or supplement your professional library.

One week before school begins, you need to prepare your teaching station by posting rules and other signs and by creating an attractive bulletin board. You must place class rosters into a grade book as well as a computer spreadsheet program. At this time, you should also create a substitute folder, review lesson plans and the first unit of instruction, and prepare a beginning-of-school letter to be sent home to parents or guardians. On the first day of school, you must dress professionally, be punctual, and above all, be enthusiastic.

DISCUSSION QUESTIONS

1. Why is it important to inspect facilities and equipment before the school year?

2. Why is creating a professional library important? What resources will you include in your professional library?

3. What actions will you take before the school year begins to get to know your students?

4. What are your professional responsibilities as a physical educator and why are they important?

Checklist for Personal Employment Folder

_____ Copy of contract

_____ School roster

_____ District roster

_____ Benefit forms

_____ Copies of professional memberships

_____ District calendar

_____ Employee handbook

_____ Current resume

_____ Copy of teaching certification

_____ Documentation of professional development activities

_____ List of professional goals

From A. James, 2013, *Survive and thrive as a physical educator: Strategies for the first year and beyond* (Champaign, IL: Human Kinetics).

School and District Roster

Position	Name	Phone	E-mail
Principal			
Assistant principal			
Custodian			
Secretary			
Nurse			
Substitute caller (the person you should call when you will be absent from school because of an illness or unforeseen emergency)			
Counselor			
Music or band teacher			
Grade level teachers (elementary level)			
Subject teachers (secondary level)			
Art teacher			
Librarian			
Technology teacher			
Speech therapist			
Physical therapist			
Paraeducators			
Director of physical education			
Director of physical education's secretary			
Athletic director (if different from the director of physical education)			
Athletic director's secretary			
Superintendent			
Superintendent's secretary			
Assistant superintendent			
Assistant superintendent's secretary			

From A. James, 2013, *Survive and thrive as a physical educator: Strategies for the first year and beyond* (Champaign, IL: Human Kinetics).

RESOURCE 2.3

Equipment Inventory and Assessment

Equipment	Number	CONDITION		
		Excellent	Good	Fair

Facilities Assessment

Indoor space	CONDITION			
	Excellent	Good	Fair	Safety concerns
Outdoor space	CONDITION			
	Excellent	Good	Fair	Safety concerns

From A. James, 2013, *Survive and thrive as a physical educator: Strategies for the first year and beyond* (Champaign, IL: Human Kinetics).

Substitute Teacher Feedback Form

Dear Substitute:

Thank you for subbing in my physical education classes today while I was absent. I would appreciate any feedback that you can provide me concerning my classes today. Please use the following form to provide feedback. In addition, feel free to write any comments you may have on the form.

Sincerely,

[Teacher's name]

SUBSTITUTE FEEDBACK FORM

Substitute teacher's name:_____

Substitute teacher's contact information (phone and e-mail):

_____

1. Briefly describe how the day went.

2. Please comment on your success with implementing the lesson plans.

3. Please comment on any students who were particularly helpful.

4. Please comment on any issues or behavior problems that you had with specific students.

5. Please share any other information that you believe I need to know about your day.

From A. James, 2013, *Survive and thrive as a physical educator: Strategies for the first year and beyond* (Champaign, IL: Human Kinetics).

Sample "Get to Know You" Questionnaire

Student's name: _____

Nickname or another name you would like to be called: _____
_____

Your pet (if any): _____

What do you like to do when you are not in school? _____
_____

What sports do you like? _____
_____

What are your hobbies? _____
_____

Do you play an instrument or sing? _____
_____

What makes you different from others? _____
_____

Who is your favorite musical artist? _____
_____

What is your favorite television show? _____
_____

What is your favorite sport team? _____
_____

What is your favorite movie? _____
_____

Names of brothers or sisters (if any): _____
_____

Names of parents or guardians: _____
_____

From A. James, 2013, *Survive and thrive as a physical educator: Strategies for the first year and beyond* (Champaign, IL: Human Kinetics).

CHAPTER 3

Preparing Unit and Lesson Plans

Creating unit and lesson plans is a very important skill that you need to master and use throughout your career. By planning effective units and lessons, you create blueprints that lead to student learning, as well as the attainment of learning standards. As the saying goes, failing to plan means planning to fail. This statement is true in all aspects of life but is particularly salient for a teacher. As a student, you probably resented the time and labor that you had to put into assignments that involved planning for instruction; however, the practice and attention to detail will serve you well as a teacher.

A common mistake for many teachers, both novice and veteran, is not spending enough time planning for instructional units and lessons. Successful teachers plan and assess for learning each day they teach. You must dedicate the time necessary to plan lessons and units that provide for sequential instruction and that lead to the achievement of student learning outcomes. Of course, you will face certain planning problems that veteran teachers have solved through their experience. This chapter addresses several of these problems and covers specific topics that will help you become a skilled teacher who plans for student learning. These topics include unit planning, content development, and instructional approaches.

Understanding the Planning Process: Seeing the Big Picture

Before you develop unit plans and daily lesson plans, you must have a vision for what the students need to learn by the end of the school year. To do this, you must create a full-year plan for each grade level that you will teach. You will need to review your district curriculum, as well as the state and national standards. The national standards can be found on the website of the American Alliance for Health, Physical Education, Recreation and Dance (www.aahperd.org/naspe/standards/nationalstandards/PEstandards.cfm). If your state has standards for physical education, you can probably find them on the website for the state's department of education.

After you have reviewed your district curriculum and the state and national standards, you should review your methods textbooks as well as books and websites that deal with physical education content. Appendix B provides a list of websites and books that will be beneficial for you to review. Make sure that you set aside time to review these resources carefully before the school year begins.

The final thing to do before preparing full-year plans is to talk with your colleagues. As a beginning teacher, you do not have a lot of unit and lesson plans of your own, so it is important to ask other teachers to share resources and ideas with you. Remember, if you borrow resources, you must be sure to return them and to personally thank your colleagues (either verbally or with a written note) for sharing the materials with you.

Full-Year Plan

After reviewing the curriculum guide, standards, and resources, you will have an idea of what should be taught at each grade level throughout the year. The content of the full-year plan is called the scope, and the order it is placed in is called the sequence. The sequence provides an overview of the order in which the content will be taught at each grade level.

Next, you need to create a full-year plan for each grade level that you will be teaching. The full-year plan will serve as a guide for planning throughout the year and will make unit and lesson planning easier and more efficient. The easiest way to develop a full-year plan is to create a calendar for the school year that documents teaching days as well as days off for holidays or school obligations (such as superintendent days or parent–teacher conferences). In addition to placing teaching days onto the calendar, you should also specify days for teaching specific units. Here is a step-by-step process for creating a full-year plan:

▶ **Step 1.** Review the following resources: (a) curriculum guides, (b) state and national standards, (c) methods textbooks, and (d) other content books and web resources.

▶ **Step 2.** Decide on the units you will teach at each grade level and the length of the units.

▶ **Step 3.** Create a calendar of the school year for each grade level.

▶ **Step 4.** Write the days you will teach onto the calendar. Also specify the days on which there will be no instruction.

▶ **Step 5.** Write each unit and the days you will teach each unit onto the calendar.

▶ **Step 6.** On the calendar, note any resources such as books, videos, or websites that you may use to plan the unit.

Be sure to place the units that you want to teach into a logical order that not only provides enough days for students to learn the content but also builds on students' prior knowledge and skill levels. For example, for teaching basketball, you should develop a unit that includes advanced skills such as the crossover and spin dribble rather than teach basic dribbling to students who are already competent in basic dribbling skills. All too often, physical education teachers teach the same skills every year, which leads to a lack of student motivation and a lack of learning. Furthermore, you need to plan content in the beginning of the year that is challenging and developmentally appropriate. This helps ensure that your students will become confident movers and will be excited to take part in physical education.

Unit Plans

After creating full-year plans, you need to create unit plans that align with the full-year plan. Developing a complete and detailed unit plan is essential for effective teaching and student learning. Figure 3.1 serves as a guide for unit planning. In addition, resource 3.1 provides a useful template for unit planning.

When creating unit plans, you must first determine the number of days the unit will cover, which is included in the full-year plan. The length of time you plan to spend on a unit will serve as a guide for the number and type of activities that will be included in the unit.

In planning the unit, you must be sure to write developmentally appropriate learning objectives for the unit. Learning objectives serve as the basis for the design of the unit. Well-written objectives for a unit provide a clear purpose for both the teacher and the student. Based on unit objectives, students are able to evaluate their performance and concentrate on areas needing improvement. Teachers can use unit

1. _____ Determine the length of the unit.

2. _____ Write learning objectives.

3. _____ Create a block plan that determines the sequence of the content for the unit.

4. _____ Determine how students' skill and knowledge will be preassessed.

5. _____ Create an assessment plan.

6. _____ Create assessments.

7. _____ Draft daily lesson plans.

8. _____ Place the unit plan in a binder to keep it organized.

▶ **FIGURE 3.1** Unit planning checklist.

objectives to assess progress toward the objectives and to determine the extent to which students have achieved the objectives (Buck, Lund, Harrison, & Cook, 2007).

Next, you should create a block plan that consists of developmentally appropriate content that demonstrates a gradual progression within and across the days of the unit. The block plan should also include a learning focus for each day, the equipment that is needed, and the assessments for specific days.

The first day of the block plan should include a preassessment to determine students' skill levels and prior knowledge. The type of preassessment will depend on the learning objectives and the developmental level of students. For example, at the middle school level, a teacher may want to preassess students' volleyball skills and may be unsure of students' prior experience with volleyball. The teacher may decide to preassess students' skills using stations such as overhead pass, forehand pass, underhand serve, and a station where students take a written quiz.

Each of your unit objectives will need to be assessed in some manner. As part of the unit planning process, you must create an assessment plan for the unit that aligns with the learning objectives for the unit. An assessment plan consists of the following:

▶ Learning objectives for the unit

▶ Specific criteria that will be assessed for each objective

▶ Assessment tools that are used as a preassessment or in a formative or summative manner

▶ The days on which the assessments will take place

▶ Any accommodations you will make for the assessments, such as lowering the nets in a volleyball unit

Assessment and the creation of an assessment plan will be discussed in more detail in chapter 4. In addition, that chapter provides a sample assessment plan.

The next step is to create the assessments to be used in the unit. It may seem odd to create assessments for an entire unit before creating daily lesson plans; however, if you do this after creating your block plan and writing unit objectives, your unit will be instructionally aligned (i.e., assessments align with learning activities and objectives), which leads to more student learning (Cohen, 1987). Instructional alignment and the impact that it has on student learning will be discussed in detail in chapter 4.

Finally, you need to create drafts of daily lesson plans as part of your unit plan. It is better to write out drafts of daily plans for the entire unit so that changes can be made to lesson plans as the unit progresses.

▶ Successful teachers dedicate time to create detailed unit plans and daily lesson plans.

Lesson Plans

Lesson planning determines the core of what happens in a school day. If you want to have a successful day teaching, you must plan for it. Although the full-year plan and unit plans are the backbone of the planning process, the daily lesson plans are what make lessons come to life for your students. Daily lesson plans follow a specific format. Your school district may have a format for you to use; if not, you can create your own format or use the format that you learned in college. Resource 3.2 provides a sample format for planning lessons.

Lesson plans should be developmentally appropriate, which means that the skills match the ability of the students and provide for a gradual progression from the beginning of the lesson to the end. In addition, there are several aspects to a properly prepared lesson plan:

▶ **Anticipatory set or lesson introduction.** The purpose of the anticipatory set is to motivate students so that they become interested in the lesson and understand the purpose of the lesson.

▶ **Connection to state and national standards.** By providing a rationale for how the lesson and lesson objectives are connected to state and national standards, you will be able to demonstrate to others (i.e., administrators) that you are teaching in a manner that achieves the standards.

▶ **Lesson focus.** The lesson focus provides a description of the focal point of the lesson.

▶ **Learning objectives.** The purpose of learning objectives in a lesson plan is to determine what students should learn by the end of the lesson. A specific learning objective has an action verb, content, criteria, and a condition.

▶ **Safety.** This includes general safety concerns regarding space, flooring, or field surfaces, as well as specific safety issues pertaining to a specific unit (i.e., goggles for floor hockey).

▶ **Materials and equipment.** All necessary materials and equipment for the lesson should be identified. Always plan for more equipment than the number of students in your class.

▶ **Organization of students and equipment.** Careful consideration must be given to the organization of students and equipment during the performance of tasks. Make sure that enough space is allotted for students to perform tasks safely.

▶ **Closure.** The closure is performed at the end of the lesson to reinforce and check for understanding of the lesson objectives.

▶ **Reflection.** It is a good idea to include a short reflection on the lesson plan form in regard to student learning or your effectiveness as a teacher during the lesson. There is a space for reflection on the sample lesson plan form provided in resource 3.2.

Content Development

A large part of lesson planning is developing content. Developing content is the process of sequencing movement tasks in a manner that has the potential to facilitate learning (Rink, 2010). Teachers may develop content to make tasks easier or more difficult, to have students focus on the quality of a task, or to challenge students by providing them with opportunities to test themselves and motivating them to continue the task (Rink, 2010).

Rink (2010) provides a framework for content development in physical education. This framework consists of four types of tasks: informing, extending, refining, and applying. Informing tasks are tasks that provide students with information about the task they are about to perform. An extending task involves making a task easier or more difficult to match the developmental level of students. A refining task is a task that focuses on the quality of performance or the proper technique. Finally, application tasks are used to challenge students and maintain their interest in a task. You must use these tasks to develop content that will lead to student learning and the attainment of student learning outcomes. There is no set sequence of extending, refining, and application tasks. After presenting the initial task, you need to decide what to do based on what you see (Rink, 2010).

For example, if you are developing content related to the skill of throwing overhand to a target for an elementary level lesson, the informing task could be to have students throw overhand at a target on the wall that is 15 feet way. To refine the task in a manner that would have students focus on the quality of the task, you could ask them to throw at the target but to focus on their follow-through by pointing their fingers at the target. To make the task more difficult, you could ask the students to move two giant steps back so they are throwing from a farther distance. Finally, to provide an application task, you could ask students to count the number of times they are able to hit the target in a specific amount of time.

These tasks can be planned for in a lesson; however, decisions regarding the implementation of these tasks are often made while observing students. As you observe students, you can determine how tasks should be changed for the entire class, small groups, or individual students based on their needs and their developmental level. By planning tasks that are easier or more difficult, or tasks that allow students to practice in a manner that enhances the quality of their performance, you will be able to make changes to tasks based on your observation of students while at the same time being engaged in the teaching process.

Although having a well-planned unit and a sound lesson plan can make teaching more effective, you will still struggle with various aspects of planning. Table 3.1 presents problems associated with planning that beginning teachers often face, along with solutions based on the information that has been presented in this chapter.

Instructional Approaches

In addition to planning sequential instruction that leads to student learning, you have to choose the proper instructional approach in order to deliver content in an effective manner. You have several instructional approaches to choose from depending on the goals of the lesson, including direct instruction, peer teaching, task teaching, guided discovery, and cooperative learning.

TABLE 3.1

Planning Problems and Possible Solutions

Problem	Possible solution
Rushing to cover material instead of taking the time to teach and making sure students are learning	Slow down and use formative assessments to determine if students are learning. If students are not learning, go back and reteach material and give students more practice opportunities.
Failing to connect current learning to previous learning (otherwise known as scaffolding)	Make efforts to provide connections to previous learning in the anticipatory set and closure of lessons.
Not differentiating instruction	Use a variety of tasks, especially tasks that are extended up or down to accommodate different ability levels.
Failing to provide an anticipatory set that excites and captures students' attention	Ask questions about specific tactics, tell a story, or ask students about their experiences with an activity in order to get students excited about the upcoming lesson.
Failing to assess and evaluate student learning	Create an assessment plan for each unit of instruction. The assessment plan should include formative and summative assessments that are aligned with learning outcomes.
Failing to create a yearly plan	Set time aside in the summer to create yearly plans. Yearly plans should be based on the curriculum. Yearly plans give a clear idea of what students are expected to learn.
Failing to create unit and lesson plans	Unit plans should include learning objectives, a block plan that contains content that is developmentally appropriate (with a gradual progression), an assessment plan, assessments, and lesson plans. Use a lesson plan format that is efficient and easy to use. Plan lessons around learning objectives and state and national standards. Always plan more than you believe your students will be able to finish. Keep unit and lesson plans in a binder so they can be easily accessed when needed. Set aside time each week to write and review unit and lesson plans.
Failing to provide a detailed closure related to lesson objectives	Create specific questions that can be asked during closure; these questions should align with unit objectives. Use assessments such as exit slips during closure.
Failing to preassess students to determine their knowledge and skill level	The first day of each unit should include a preassessment of the skills and knowledge that you are planning to teach. Stations are a great way to conduct a preassessment. Stations could include skill stations as well as a station that gives students a short quiz to assess their knowledge of the activity.
Failing to use assessments	Write your assessments as you write unit plans. Make creating assessments part of the planning process.

Direct instruction is one of the most commonly used instructional approaches. In this approach, you tell students what to do, show them how to practice, and then manage their practice. Students often work as a whole class or in small groups. Typically, the entire class practices the same task or some variation of that task (Graham, Holt/Hale, & Parker, 2010).

Peer teaching is an instructional approach that involves peers being paired or put into small groups in order to teach each other. As the teacher, you plan tasks and share them with students, and the students take on the role of providing feedback and assessing their partner or fellow group members. For peer teaching to be effective, the skill should be fairly simple, the cues for observation need to be very clear, and performance must be easily measured (Graham, Holt/Hale, & Parker, 2010).

Task teaching is another popular instructional approach that allows students to practice different tasks at the same time. Task teaching can include stations or task sheets. Both stations and task sheets allow students to practice different tasks at their own pace and assess their

▶ Many physical education teachers use the direct instruction approach, in which they tell students what to do and manage their practice.

performance against specific criteria. Resource 3.3 provides an example of a task sheet for jump roping. For task teaching to be effective, you need to explain and demonstrate the stations and task sheets before students practice. In addition, you must explain how students should rotate as well as where and how they are supposed to leave the equipment at each station. Stations are often used at the end of a unit to review tasks that have been previously taught in the unit (Graham, Holt/Hale, & Parker, 2010).

Guided discovery is an approach in which you guide students through a task by asking questions. You describe how the task is to be practiced and a way to measure success, but it is left to the student to decide how to perform the task. Teachers use two types of guided discovery: convergent and divergent inquiry. In convergent inquiry, you ask a series of questions and persuade students to find the same answer. Divergent inquiry, on the other hand, challenges the students to find many answers to a task or problem posed by the teacher (Graham, Holt/ Hale, & Parker, 2010).

The final approach is cooperative learning. Cooperative learning is an instructional approach that promotes group interdependence and individual responsibility on behalf of students. Three cooperative learning techniques that are often used in physical education are jigsaw, pairs check, and co-op (Graham, Holt/Hale, & Parker, 2010). The jigsaw technique involves small groups of students. Each student in the group becomes an "expert" on a specific skill. For example, in learning a four-part dance, each student in a group of four could become an expert on one specific part of the dance. The experts would each teach their part of the dance to their group, and the group would combine all four parts to perform the entire dance.

Pairs check is a technique that involves students in groups of four. Each group of four is split into two pairs. Each pair of partners practices a task, employing the peer teaching approach. The two partner pairs then get together and assess each other, providing feedback to help enhance the other pair's practice of the skill. The partner pairs then continue to practice using the feedback provided by the other pair of partners (Graham, Holt/Hale, & Parker, 2010).

Co-op is a cooperative learning technique in which several small groups are used to create a project with many components. Each group is responsible for one component of the larger project (Graham, Holt/ Hale, & Parker, 2010). The co-op approach works well with an activity that includes several elements.

For example, the dancing homework machine is a co-op activity that splits students into five groups. Each group performs one of the functions of the homework machine: (a) the in slot; (b) smoothers; (c) computers; (d) homework checkers; and (e) the out slot. Each group creates a repetitive sequence of three movements that they perform in unison to represent the part of the homework machine that they are assigned. Each movement is performed for eight counts.

▶ The group that represents the in slot would create movements that repeat a reaching and pulling movement to pull the homework into the machine. The movement sequence should begin small and get bigger each time the movement is changed.

▶ The smoother group would create movements that show how they would smooth out the crumpled homework. Each movement should be at a different level and should use a different body part.

▶ The computer group needs to create movements that represent the inside of a working computer. The group should pick movements that use the whole body, and the movements should be very big or exaggerated.

▶ The homework checkers need to create movements that demonstrate that the homework is done correctly. The group should create movements that change with every eight beats of the drum and indicate that the homework has been checked and is complete. An example would be a movement that represents placing a stamp on the homework.

▶ Finally, the last part of the machine is the out slot. This group would create movements that represent pushing the homework out of the machine. The movements could involve using different forces such as light and hard as well as using different body parts to push.

Each group practices their sequence of three movements. They then practice the sequence to the external beat of the drum. At the end of the practice with the external beat, the teacher has all of the groups come together and practice their sequence of movements as one large group, changing each movement in their sequence every eight beats. The teacher then plays music, and the students clap the beat that the homework machine must move to. Afterward, the teacher plays music, and students perform their movement sequences to put all of the movements of the homework machine together (Cone & Cone, 2005).

Summary

Planning for student learning is a significant aspect of a physical education teacher's job. You must take time to plan units of instruction and daily lesson plans with attention to detail. Moreover, a lesson with good content development promotes student learning and involvement. In addition, to enhance the teaching-learning process, you should use various instructional approaches, such as direct instruction, peer teaching, guided discovery, task teaching, and cooperative learning.

DISCUSSION QUESTIONS

1. Why is planning important?

2. What is a full-year plan and why is it a necessary aspect of planning?

3. What is content development? How does content development contribute to student learning?

4. What instructional approaches can teachers use in their instruction? Why should a teacher use different instructional approaches?

Sample Unit Planning Template

Unit: _____   Duration of unit: _____   Grade level: _____

Unit objectives: _____

_____

BLOCK PLAN

For each day, specify the focus, the content, the assessments to be used, and the equipment and resources needed.

Day 1	Day 2	Day 3	Day 4	Day 5
Day 6	Day 7	Day 8	Day 9	Day 10

ASSESSMENT PLAN

Unit objective	Criteria to be assessed	Assessment tool, assessment cycle, and day of unit	Assessment adaptations	Possible points for the assessment

LESSON PLANS

(created using the lesson plan template)

From A. James, 2013, *Survive and thrive as a physical educator: Strategies for the first year and beyond* (Champaign, IL: Human Kinetics).

Sample Lesson Planning Form

Class/grade level: _____ Date: _____

Unit/theme: _____ Lesson # _____ of _____

Skills already developed by students: _____

1. Lesson focus:

2. Lesson objectives:

3. State and NASPE standards targeted:

4. Rationale for how the lesson objectives are connected to state and national learning standards:

5. Assessments aligned with objectives:

6. Modifications for students with special needs:

7. Safety concerns:

8. Equipment and resources needed:

Time	Task description and development	Student, teacher, and equipment organization	Description of teaching cues	Safety

REFLECTION:

From A. James, 2013, *Survive and thrive as a physical educator: Strategies for the first year and beyond* (Champaign, IL: Human Kinetics).

Sample Task Sheet

Directions: Practice each of the jump rope tasks in order. Find a classmate to watch you perform the jump rope task. After you perform the task, ask the classmate to initial your task sheet to verify that you were able to complete the jump rope task. Then move on to the next task. You cannot have a classmate sign your task sheet more than once.

JUMP ROPE TASK SHEET

Task	Peer's initials
1. Do 10 side swings with the jump rope.	
2. Skip your rope 10 times.	
3. Jump 10 times using a two-foot basic jump.	
4. Jump 10 times on your right foot.	
5. Jump 10 times on your left foot.	
6. Jump 10 times using a straddle jump.	
7. Jump 10 times using a scissor jump.	
8. Jump 10 times using a skier jump.	
9. Jump 5 times using a crossover jump.	
10. Jump 5 times using a double under jump.	

From A. James, 2013, *Survive and thrive as a physical educator: Strategies for the first year and beyond* (Champaign, IL: Human Kinetics).

Student Assessment and Evaluation

Assessment in physical education involves collecting, describing, and quantifying information about performance (Siedentop & Tannehill, 2000). Assessment is an essential element of the instructional process; without it, you have no way of knowing if learning has occurred or whether learning objectives have been attained, and students have no indication of how they are doing in physical education (Lund & Tannehill, 2010).

Another reason that assessment is an important part of the instructional process is because it is an integral aspect of instructional alignment. Instructional alignment occurs when assessments and learning activities match student learning objectives (Cohen, 1987). If assessment is absent from the instructional process, instructional alignment will not exist. Research results have indicated that instructionally aligned units and lessons increase student learning more than units and lessons that are not instructionally aligned (Elia, 1986; Fahey, 1986; Koczor, 1984).

As a beginning teacher, you may find that assessment has not been part of your students' prior experiences in physical education. If this is the case, the students may be very resistant to assessment. You will have to work to create a culture in the gymnasium that values assessment. You can do this in several ways. First, you must plan for and use assessments in each unit of instruction. Second, make sure you explain the importance of assessment in the learning process to students. Third, share assessment instruments with students so that they know what is expected of them in terms of their performance. Fourth, hold students accountable for their performance on the assessments by linking assessments to a grade. Finally, allow students to assume some responsibility in the assessment process through peer or self-assessment. Not only will students be more involved in the assessment process, but the process will also be more efficient.

Assessment Practices

Assessments can be both formal and informal. Formal assessments tend to be removed from real life. Although formal assessments may measure student performance, that performance cannot be generalized to other situations (Siedentop & Tannehill, 2000). Formal assessments are typically standardized, have established validity and reliability, and use either norm-referenced or criterion-referenced scoring that allows the teacher to interpret student performance (Rink, 2010). Examples of formal assessments include skill tests, written tests, and the Fitnessgram.

Informal assessment is a means of using assessment in a manner that integrates it into the learning process in order to promote student learning (Siedentop & Tannehill, 2000). Most teachers use observation as an informal means of assessing students. Teachers use a variety of assessment instruments—including checklists, rating scales, and rubrics—to record these observations. Observations made when giving oral feedback to students about their performance are not considered assessments. If observation is used as an assessment, it must produce some type of written record of the performance (Lund & Tannehill, 2010).

Throughout a unit of instruction, a physical education teacher should use an assessment cycle to monitor student learning and to enhance the teaching-learning process. The cycle includes preassessment, formative assessment, and summative assessment.

The assessment cycle in a unit begins with a preassessment of students' skills. Preassessment allows you to gather information about each student's skill level, knowledge, and attitude toward a specific activity. This information will be helpful in planning developmentally appropriate learning tasks.

The second part of the cycle involves formative assessment. Throughout the unit of instruction, you will use formative assessments as learning activities to provide feedback that will affect the ongoing instructional process (Siedentop & Tannehill, 2000). Formative assessments are assessments for learning (Lund & Tannehill, 2010). They are used to assess progress toward a goal (Rink, 2010). Formative assessments allow you to make decisions about reteaching specific content that students may be struggling with, or to continue as planned with instruction. Teachers use formative assessment in various ways in physical education:

- ▶ Allow students to assess their own performance and identify their weaknesses
- ▶ Motivate students to improve their performance
- ▶ Allow teachers to conduct an assessment regarding the effectiveness of their teaching
- ▶ Allow teachers to revise their teaching practice based on assessment information
- ▶ Provide an instructionally aligned learning experience to students
- ▶ Allow teachers to identify students who are struggling and provide guidance and feedback to help them improve

The final aspect of the assessment cycle is using summative assessment to provide a final judgment on learning (Siedentop & Tannehill, 2000). Lund and Tannehill (2010) defined summative assessment as the assessment of learning. It is intended to provide an evaluation of student learning for grading. Summative assessment determines exit success and how well students achieved the intended learning outcomes (Siedentop & Tannehill, 2000). Most summative assessments in physical education occur at the end of a unit (Rink, 2010).

Traditional Assessments

In physical education, traditional assessments such as skill tests have commonly been used to measure student progress. Historically, skill tests have been used as a formal assessment in physical education. Skill tests may be appropriate for assessing beginning skill levels or for assessing skill development of students before they use the skills in a game. Several skill tests with established validity and reliability are available to physical education teachers. Figure 4.1 lists selected references for skill tests that can be used in physical education.

Skill tests provide a way for students to practice skills in a closed environment and may motivate students to improve performance; these tests also provide students with feedback about their performance. Although skill tests have a place in physical education, they do have some limitations. For example, many published skill tests were developed for use in research projects and must be set up exactly the same way each time to ensure validity. As a result, skill tests are time

---

Racquetball skills test: Hensley, L.D., East, W.B., & Stillwell, J.L. (1979). A racquetball skills test. *Research Quarterly, 50,* 114-118.

Tennis skills test: AAHPERD. (1989). *Tennis skills test manual.* Reston, VA: American Alliance for Health, Physical Education, Recreation and Dance.

Basketball skills test: Hopkins, D.R., Shick, J., & Placek, J.J. (1994). *Basketball for boys and girls: Skills test manual.* Reston, VA: American Alliance for Health, Physical Education, Recreation and Dance.

Chapman ball control test: Chapman, N.L. (1982). Chapman ball control test: Field hockey. *Research Quarterly for Exercise and Sport, 53,* 239-242.

Softball skills test: AAHPERD. (1991). *Softball skills test manual.* Reston, VA: American Alliance for Health, Physical Education, Recreation and Dance.

▶ **FIGURE 4.1** Selected skill tests.

consuming to set up and administer in a manner that follows the test protocol. Second, skill tests are not appropriate for assessing game play ability because these tests typically assess skills out of the context of the game (Lund & Kirk, 2002). This presents a dilemma because if the goal is for students to learn and execute skills in a game setting and if the skill test is not conducted in the game setting, the test is not really valid. For example, if you want to assess the forehand pass in volleyball, you may first want to ask yourself this question: Is it appropriate to assess whether a student can pass to the wall, or is it better to assess whether the student can pass to the setter in order to set up the attack in a game of volleyball? In the end, you should give serious thought to whether a predesigned skill test really assesses what you, the teacher, want students to learn.

Written tests are useful for assessing students' cognitive knowledge in physical education. Teachers commonly use multiple-choice, true–false, and matching questions on physical education tests. Written tests can be a valuable tool when you want to know whether students have learned basic knowledge about specific activities. Miller (2006) offers some helpful tips for creating written tests:

- ▶ Allow enough time to complete test construction.
- ▶ Only include items that cover important facts, concepts, principles, or skills.
- ▶ Avoid items that provide answers to other items.
- ▶ Write test items simply and clearly.
- ▶ Write tests at the comprehension level of your students.
- ▶ Write instructions using clear, concise, and simple wording.
- ▶ Proofread the test before giving it to students.

Another traditional assessment is a fitness test, which is used to measure health-related fitness. The Fitnessgram is a very popular health-related fitness test. A Fitnessgram software program is available that explains scores to students and parents and provides activity ideas that can be used to improve specific aspects of fitness. The Fitnessgram has criterion-referenced standards that allow students to evaluate where they are in relation to the criterion and set goals (Miller, 2006). Although students may be motivated to improve their fitness level in order to reach their healthy fitness zone, the National Association for Sport and Physical Education (NASPE) recommends that teachers do not use fitness tests as a basis for determining student grades.

Fitness tests have some limitations. First, genetic factors influence the results of health-related fitness tests. Genetic variations account for most of the individual differences in response to regular exercise

▶ The Fitnessgram assessment includes a curl-up test, in which one student performs the test while a partner keeps count and watches for form errors.

that develops health-related fitness components. In addition, students' genetic makeup influences how they respond or do not respond to physical activity and each aspect of health-related fitness (Bouchard, 1999). Second, age and maturation are important considerations when interpreting fitness test scores. In fact, scores on fitness tests often improve with age, even among individuals who do not exercise on a regular basis (Pangrazi & Corbin, 1990). Third, children and adolescents do not spend enough time in physical education to get the amount of activity it takes to significantly increase fitness (Corbin, 2002). Although these limitations exist, assessing health-related physical fitness can motivate students to engage in physical activity in order to become fitter.

Alternative Assessments

Although traditional assessment techniques such as skill tests are available to physical education teachers, alternative or authentic assessments have become very popular in physical education. Alternative assessments resemble "real-life" tasks and take on many forms. They focus on the use of what is learned in real-life settings. Usually, the assessment is based on observation of a performance (Rink, 2010).

Observations are a commonly used assessment in physical education. They can be done by teachers or by students through peer or self-assessment. Recording these observations in some way makes the assessment more official because it requires you to identify the critical elements of performance that are linked to the learning objectives. In addition, by recording the observations, you make an effort to observe each student and document student learning in a more systematic manner. Furthermore, this method provides better information than "eyeballing" student performance and not recording it (Rink, 2010). Common types of alternative assessments in physical education include checklists, rating scales, and rubrics.

▶ **Checklists.** You can use a checklist when you want to know if a student can perform a certain skill. Checklists require a "yes" or "no" answer. In physical education, checklists are used to determine if the student is exhibiting the critical aspects of performance or the product of performance (Rink, 2010). Resource 4.1 is an example of a checklist that could be used to evaluate throwing in an elementary physical education class.

▶ **Rating scales.** Rating scales are similar to a checklist; however, a checklist determines if a characteristic exists, while a rating scale is used to determine the degree to which the characteristic exists (Rink, 2010). In other words, a rating scale can indicate that a student steps toward the target most of the time, but not always, whereas a checklist does not have that flexibility.

Information from a rating scale is helpful to students and teachers alike. This information can be used to give specific feedback for improvement. A rating scale can also provide information to the teacher about adjustments that need to be made to the instructional process. Resource 4.2 is an example of a rating scale for evaluating throwing.

▶ **Rubrics.** Scoring rubrics are similar to rating scales in that they examine the quality of skills; however, a scoring rubric allows you to observe different dimensions of behavior at the same time. Several steps need to be taken to create a simple rubric. The first step is to create a specific learning objective. The second step is to use the criteria of the learning objective as the criteria in the rubric. The criteria will stay the same at each level of the rubric.

The third step is to decide on the levels of performance within the rubric. Rubrics can have from three to five levels of performance. Three-level rubrics are the simplest to construct because it is easier to distinguish between levels of performance. As the number of levels of performance increases, differentiating between the levels becomes more difficult.

The final step is to decide on the indicators for each level. In a three-level rubric, the top level and desired performance on the rubric could be characterized by the indicator "always," and the least acceptable performance would be characterized by the indicator "rarely." Although "never" is frequently used as an indicator in rubrics, this may give students the message that it is acceptable to never perform the skill with the criteria the teacher has identified. By using "rarely" as the least acceptable indicator, you force the students to work to meet the minimally acceptable level of skill performance. Resource 4.3 is an example of a three-level rubric that could be used at the elementary level.

Several other assessment tools are available to physical education teachers, including student journals, portfolios, open-response questions, event tasks, and game play assessments such as the Game Performance Assessment Instrument (GPAI). The GPAI is an assessment that was developed as a comprehensive assessment tool for teachers to use and adapt for a variety of games. The GPAI allows teachers to assess performance behaviors, including the ability to solve tactical problems, move appropriately, and execute skills (Mitchell, Oslin, & Griffin, 2006). However, you should focus on a small number of assessments, such as those discussed in this chapter. As you master these assessments, you can begin to explore other assessment options that are available. Additional assessments can be further investigated by examining various resources such as the following books:

- ▶ *AAHPERD assessment series.* Reston, VA: National Association for Sport and Physical Education, an Association of the American Alliance for Health, Physical Education, Recreation and Dance.
- ▶ Collins, D.R., & Hodges, P.B. (2001). *A comprehensive guide to sports skills tests and measurement.* Lanham, MD: The Scarecrow Press, Inc.
- ▶ Hopple, C.J. (2005). *Elementary physical education teaching & assessment. A practical guide* (2nd ed.). Champaign, IL: Human Kinetics.
- ▶ Lund, J.L., & Kirk, M.F. (2010). *Performance-based assessment for middle and high school physical education* (2nd ed.). Champaign, IL: Human Kinetics.
- ▶ McGee, R., & Farrow, A. (1987). *Test questions for physical education activities.* Champaign, IL: Human Kinetics.
- ▶ Mitchell, S.A., Oslin, J.L., & Griffin, L.L. (2006). *Teaching sport concepts and skills: A tactical games approach* (2nd ed.). Champaign, IL: Human Kinetics.
- ▶ Schiemer, S. (2000). *Assessment strategies for elementary physical education.* Champaign, IL: Human Kinetics.

▸ Strand, B.N., & Wilson, R. (1993). *Assessing sport skills.* Champaign, IL: Human Kinetics.

Implementation of Assessments in Physical Education

Physical education teachers have three ways to implement assessments: teacher assessments, peer assessments, and student self-assessments. As the teacher, it is very difficult for you to conduct all assessments. Peer and self-assessments completed by students make the assessment process more efficient and relieve some of the stress placed on you to conduct all assessments.

For peer and self-assessments to work, students must be taught how to assess. The physical education teacher must provide very specific criteria for students to assess and must offer opportunities for them to practice observing and assessing these criteria during physical activities. Initially, students may only be able to observe and assess one criterion of a skill at a time; however, as students become more skillful in observing and assessing skills, they should be able to assess more than one criterion at a time.

Grading in Physical Education

Grades are marks that are used for various purposes, such as communicating with parents or guardians about the progress of their child. Grades are also used to inform students of their progress and to hold them accountable for achievement in physical education. In addition, administrators use grades to make decisions related to promotion, graduation, academic honors, and athletic eligibility. They also use grades to determine if students have met educational objectives (Miller, 2006).

In the past, physical education teachers have been reluctant to base grades on student achievement. This has been somewhat problematic because physical education grades that have been based on criteria such as being prepared and participation have led many individuals to view physical education as glorified recess. If physical education is going to be a valued subject that is equal to other academic subjects, physical education grades should be based on achievement of student learning objectives, just as grades in other academic subjects are (Lund & Kirk, 2010).

Teachers often use practices such as grading based on dress and participation, effort, or improvement; however, there are problems associated with these techniques. First, grading solely on dress and

▶ Grade students on how well they achieve the lesson's learning objectives, not on their dress, participation, effort, or improvement.

participation minimizes physical education, resulting in students perceiving that physical education is not an important subject. Dressing for participation is important because students who dress to participate are able to take part in planned assessment tasks that contribute to their grade; the grades of students who do not dress will be negatively affected. Although dressing to participate is important, it should be an expectation, rather than a large piece of a student's grade.

Grading on effort also presents a host of issues. First, effort is difficult to quantify. For example, a teacher may observe a student who appears to be putting forth effort, but as soon as the teacher moves away from the student, the student may cease to participate. A student who participates in this manner is known as a competent bystander (Siedentop & Tannehill, 2000). Another problem with grading on effort is that students who are overweight may appear to not be putting forth a great deal of effort; however, as a result of their additional weight, they may in fact be putting forth more effort than their classmates. The only way to truly measure effort is to use heart rate monitors to track student effort on an individual basis.

Finally, grading on improvement is also problematic. For example, students who are less skilled experience a great deal of improvement, while the higher skilled students do not. Thus, if a teacher graded on improvement, the lower skilled students would receive higher grades than the higher skilled students. Another issue with grading on improvement is that higher skilled students may purposely perform poorly on a pretest and then make amazing gains in their score on the posttest, which would demonstrate a great deal of improvement and result in a high grade. The final issue is that although students may improve, they may not meet the learning objectives set forth by the teacher and may not develop the desired level of competence by the end of the unit (Lund & Kirk, 2010).

A grade in physical education should report the achievement of a student and should represent the degree to which the student has achieved course objectives (Lund & Kirk, 2010). Keep this principle in mind when determining a grading philosophy. Although it may be tempting to follow traditional grading practices that are inappropriate (such as grading on dress and attendance, effort, and improvement), student grades should be determined based on the degree to which the students have met course objectives.

To assign grades that represent whether or not a student has achieved course objectives, you need to develop a grading philosophy based on the goals of the program. Note that grading philosophies may vary based on curricular and unit outcomes; however, a grading philosophy should include all three domains: psychomotor, cognitive, and affective. For example, a program that emphasizes the psychomotor domain may indicate that 60 percent of the student grade comes from the psychomotor domain, 30 percent comes from the cognitive domain, and 10 percent comes from the affective domain.

When planning a unit of instruction, you should create an assessment plan that includes unit assessments that are not only weighted in line with the grading philosophy but also aligned with learning objectives. Resource 4.4 provides an example of an assessment plan for a middle school volleyball unit. Note that not all assessments have to be used to determine a grade. Formative assessments, as described earlier, are used as assessments for learning and may not contribute to the final grade for a specific unit.

A teacher can create a grading plan using the assessments included in the assessment plan. Figure 4.2 presents an example of a grading plan for a middle school volleyball unit that aligns with the assessment plan in resource 4.4. The figure includes a detailed description of the grading plan for all three domains.

Program Goal Percentages for Learning Domains

Psychomotor = 60%
Cognitive = 30%
Affective = 10%

PSYCHOMOTOR ASSESSMENTS

Five assessments worth 12% each = 60%

	Points possible
1. Forearm pass rubric	12
2. Overhand pass rubric	12
3. Underhand serve rubric	12
4. Dig rubric	12
5. Game play assessment	12
Total points possible	**60 points**

COGNITIVE ASSESSMENTS

Three assessments worth 10% each = 30%

	Points possible
1. Written test	10
2. Student project (trifold)	10
3. Journal	10
Total points possible	**30 points**

AFFECTIVE ASSESSMENTS

One assessment worth 10% = 10%

	Points possible
1. Sporting behavior rubric	10
Total points possible	**10 points**

▶ **FIGURE 4.2** Sample grading plan for a middle school volleyball unit.

A grade can be determined from the grading plan in figure 4.2 in the following fashion. Each of the five psychomotor assessments is worth 12 percent for a total of 60 percent. Take the score on each assessment and multiply it by .12 to determine the points earned on each assessment. Each of the three cognitive assessments is worth 10 percent for a total of 30 percent of the grade. To determine the points for the cognitive domain, the same procedure is followed; however, the score on each assessment should be multiplied by .10. Finally, the one assessment in the affective domain is worth 10 percent. Again, the same procedure should be followed, and the score on the assessment should be multiplied by .10.

Figure 4.3 provides an example of how to determine a grade from the grading plan in figure 4.2. The grade for the student in the example would be 86.7 (52.2 + 24.5 + 10), which would result in a grade of B+.

Grades are typically reported for a quarter, which usually covers nine weeks of instruction. Depending on the length of the units, a teacher may cover two or three units per quarter. For each student, the teacher would determine a grade for each unit. To determine a student's grade for the quarter, the teacher would calculate the average for the student's grades for the two or three units. For example, let's say a student had the following grades for a quarter: (a) basketball unit = 85; (b) ice skating unit = 90; and (c) volleyball unit = 87. This student's grade for the quarter would be 87.3, which would be reported as a B+ on the report card.

Although the previous example is useful in determining grades at the middle school or high school level, it may or may not be applicable at the elementary level. Grades in elementary schools may or may not be based on a numeric scale. Elementary grades are sometimes determined using a system based on the level to which students are meeting state or national standards. In addition, some elementary schools may use a check, plus, or minus system. A check would indicate that students are on target, a plus would mean that they are exceeding the target, and a minus would indicate that they are not meeting the target. Other grading systems that use indicators such as excellent, satisfactory, and unsatisfactory are also popular in elementary schools.

Even though grades are determined differently in elementary schools, you still need to perform assessments and document student learning in order to have evidence to support a grade. To provide this documentation, you need to create and implement an assessment plan to assess student learning. The process described earlier for determining a grade based on an assessment plan is still applicable at the elementary level; however, adjustments may need to be made. One adjustment would be to determine a grading scale that aligns with the manner in which your school reports grades. For example, if grades are reported as excellent, satisfactory, or unsatisfactory, you could create a grading scale in which 87 to 100 percent equals excellent, 73 to 86 percent equals satisfactory, and below 73 percent equals unsatisfactory.

Program Goal Percentages for Learning Domains

Psychomotor = 60%
Cognitive = 30%
Affective = 10%

PSYCHOMOTOR ASSESSMENTS

Five assessments worth 12% each = 60%

	Assessment score	Points awarded
1. Forearm pass rubric	3/4	75 × .12 = 9
2. Overhand pass rubric	4/4	100 × .12 = 12
3. Underhand serve rubric	4/4	100 × .12 = 12
4. Dig rubric	3/4	75 × .12 = 9
5. Game play assessment	10/12	85 × .12 = 10.2
Total points awarded		**52.2 points**

COGNITIVE ASSESSMENTS

Three assessments worth 10% each = 30%

	Assessment score	Points awarded
1. Written test	90%	90 × .10 = 9
2. Student project (trifold)	85%	85 × .10 = 8.5
3. Journal	70%	70 × .10 = 7
Total points awarded		**24.5 points**

AFFECTIVE ASSESSMENTS

One assessment worth 10% = 10%

	Assessment score	Points awarded
1. Sporting behavior rubric	4/4	100 × .10 = 10
Total points awarded		**10 points**
Total points for unit		**86.7 points**
Grade for unit		**B+**

▶ **FIGURE 4.3** Determining a grade from the grading plan.

Summary

Assessment is an essential piece of the planning process. Assessments can be formal or informal; however, teachers must ensure that assessments align with the learning objectives put forth for a unit of instruction. In addition, assessments can be formative or summative.

Each unit of instruction should include an assessment plan and a grading plan. The assessment plan includes unit objectives as well as assessments that are aligned with those objectives. Moreover, the assessments on the assessment plan should reflect the assessment cycle—that is, preassessments, formative assessments, and summative assessments should be included.

A grading plan should be based on all three domains and on the assessments included in the unit assessment plan. The three domains should be weighted in a manner that reflects the philosophy of the physical education program.

DISCUSSION QUESTIONS

1. Why should physical education teachers use assessment?

2. What is instructional alignment and why is it important?

3. What are the parts of the assessment cycle? Define the three parts of the assessment cycle.

4. What is the difference between formal and informal assessment?

5. What is the difference between alternative and traditional assessments?

6. What factors should be considered in grading?

Throwing Checklist

Specific performance objective: The student will be able to demonstrate an overhead throw (side to target, arm way back, step with opposite foot, follow through) to a target 20 feet away.

Name	Side to target	Arm way back	Step with opposite foot	Follow through to target
	YES or NO	YES or NO	YES or NO	YES or NO

From A. James, 2013, *Survive and thrive as a physical educator: Strategies for the first year and beyond* (Champaign, IL: Human Kinetics).

Rating Scale for Throwing

Specific performance objective: The student will be able to demonstrate an overhead throw (side to target, arm way back, step with opposite foot, follow through) to a target 20 feet away.

Name	Side to target	Arm way back	Step with opposite foot	Follow through
	Rate on scale of 1 to 5 (1 = rarely; 5 = always)	Rate on scale of 1 to 5 (1 = rarely; 5 = always)	Rate on scale of 1 to 5 (1 = rarely; 5 = always)	Rate on scale of 1 to 5 (1 = rarely; 5 = always)

From A. James, 2013, *Survive and thrive as a physical educator: Strategies for the first year and beyond* (Champaign, IL: Human Kinetics).

Three-Level Rubric for Throwing

Specific performance objective: The student will be able to demonstrate an overhead throw (side to target, arm way back, step with opposite foot, follow through) to a target 20 feet away.

3. When throwing, student *always* has side to target, moves arm way back, steps with opposite foot, and follows through.

2. When throwing, student *sometimes* has side to target, moves arm way back, steps with opposite foot, and follows through.

1. When throwing, student *rarely* has side to target, moves arm way back, steps with opposite foot, and follows through.

Name	Rubric score

From A. James, 2013, *Survive and thrive as a physical educator: Strategies for the first year and beyond* (Champaign, IL: Human Kinetics).

Assessment Plan for Middle School Volleyball

Total Weighting:

Psychomotor = 60%   Cognitive = 30%   Affective = 10%

Unit objective	Criteria to be assessed	Assessment tool, assessment cycle, and day of unit	Assessment adaptations	Possible points for the assessment
1. The student will be able to demonstrate the forearm pass (feet to ball, flat platform, belly button to target) in a game situation.	Feet to ball Flat platform Belly button to target	Rubric; preassessment (day 1) Checklist; formative (day 2) Rubric; summative (days 8 and 9)	Lower net Use trainer volleyballs	12
2. The student will be able to demonstrate the overhand pass (volleyball shaped hands at forehead, push ball out, square to target) in a game situation.	Volleyball shaped hands at forehead Push ball out Square to target	Rubric; preassessment (day 1) Checklist; formative (day 3) Rubric; summative (days 8 and 9)	Lower net Use trainer volleyballs	12
3. The student will be able to demonstrate the underhand serve (step in opposition, hit out of hand, follow through toward target) in a game situation.	Step in opposition Hit out of hand Follow through toward target	Rubric; preassessment (day 1) Checklist; formative (day 4) Rubric; summative (days 8 and 9)	Lower net Use trainer volleyballs	12

(continued)

Unit objective	Criteria to be assessed	Assessment tool, assessment cycle, and day of unit	Assessment adaptations	Possible points for the assessment
4. The student will be able to demonstrate a forearm pass dig (don't swing arms, platform underneath ball) in a game situation.	Don't swing arms Platform underneath ball	Checklist; formative (day 6) Rubric; summative (days 8 and 9)	Lower net Use trainer volleyballs	12
5. The student will be able to demonstrate appropriate tactics (setting up attack, calling ball, defending space) in a 3v3 game.	Set up attack Call ball Defend space	Game play assessment; summative (days 8 and 9)	Lower net Use trainer volleyballs	12
6. The student will be able to identify rules (illegal hits, out of bounds), team strategies (use all three hits to set up attack, communicate), and individual strategies (front-row hitters stay away from net, call ball on defense) on a written exam.	Illegal hits Out of bounds Use all three hits Communicate Front-row hitters stay off net Call ball on defense	Written exam; summative (day 8)	Read test to nonreaders	10

7. The student will be able to evaluate community resources available for volleyball (cost, accessibility, quality of facility and equipment) on a computer-generated trifold handout.	Cost Accessibility Quality of facility and equipment	Computer-generated trifold handout (day 9)	None	10
8. The student will be able to identify and discuss his or her sporting behavior and that of teammates (teamwork, communication) in a journal.	Teamwork Communication	Journal: summative (days 1 to 9)	None	10
9. The student will be able to demonstrate sporting behavior (use positive language, compliment good play, and be encouraging) in a game situation.	Use positive language Compliment good play Be encouraging	Rubric: formative (day 4) Rubric: summative (day 8)	None	10

From A. James, 2013, *Survive and thrive as a physical educator: Strategies for the first year and beyond* (Champaign, IL: Human Kinetics).

CHAPTER 5

Classroom and Behavior Management

Maintaining discipline in the physical education classroom may be a concern for you. Perhaps you fear that you will not be able to manage classroom tasks and student behavior at the same time. Or maybe you don't have a solid understanding of what your building administrator expects in terms of classroom management and how you are supposed to deal with student behavior issues. One suggestion to help alleviate this concern is to have a conversation with your building administrator. Be sure to ask for a copy of the code of discipline. Also ask for details about what is expected in terms of classroom management and student behavior. For the most part, your building administrator will expect you to do the following:

▶ Prevent as many behavior problems as you can.
▶ Teach and enforce school rules.
▶ Develop, teach, and enforce gymnasium rules.
▶ Handle most of your own discipline problems, but refer students to an administrator if warranted by the code of discipline.
▶ Document all behavior issues and keep files up to date.

This chapter discusses several issues related to classroom management and the maintenance of appropriate student behavior. Topics include the development of rules, routines, and expectations as well as the development of a classroom management plan. In addition, the chapter covers how to promote positive student behavior and how to address student misbehavior through the use of reactive strategies and negative consequences.

Maintaining Accurate Records of Discipline

You should use a discipline log to document student misbehavior and to track the manner in which you addressed the misbehavior. This practice enables you to track the frequency and severity of student misbehavior, and it helps you reflect on the effectiveness of your methods for dealing with student misbehavior. Furthermore, this documentation is important when you are discussing possible solutions to address reoccurring or severe student misbehavior with administrators or parents.

Writing daily in a discipline log will provide you with documentation of inappropriate student behavior and your responses to misbehavior. Keeping this log will also help you to be a better teacher by allowing you to reflect on your reactions to student misbehavior as well as the strategies you employed to address student misbehavior. As you keep the log, reflect on the most frequent behavior problems you encounter and what strategies were successful in dealing with them. In addition, you should think about what content you were teaching and what instructional techniques you were using at the time of the misbehavior. Consider whether your actions may have contributed to the misbehavior. Resource 5.1 provides a template for a discipline log.

Rules, Routines, and Expectations

The goal of classroom management is to establish and maintain positive classroom procedures that minimize behavior problems. Establishing a positive learning environment will play a large role in classroom management and preventing discipline problems. One of the first steps in establishing a positive learning environment is to create rules, routines, and expectations for your classes.

Rules

Rules should be considered the laws of the gymnasium, and they must make sense to students (Graham, Holt/Hale, & Parker, 2010). Specific guidelines for creating rules for the gymnasium include the following:

▶ Keep rules few in number.
▶ State rules positively.
▶ Post rules for students to see.
▶ Keep rules flexible enough to cover various situations.
▶ Create consequences for rule breaking that are easy to carry out.
▶ Apply consequences for rule breaking fairly.

Here are some examples of common rules in physical education:

▶ Speak to classmates and teachers with respect; do not hurt people's feelings. Put-downs and teasing are inappropriate.
▶ Keep your hands and feet to yourself. It is inappropriate to touch classmates.
▶ Demonstrate good sporting behavior.
▶ Use positive language.
▶ Always follow directions.

You must discuss with students why rules are needed, provide explanations for each rule, and explain how rules will help the class run smoothly. You should teach students the rules and then use positive reinforcement when students follow the rules. By seeing the rules demonstrated and having discussions about the rules, students come to understand the rules and the behaviors that are expected.

Some teachers have their students help generate classroom rules. Getting students involved in the process of making rules helps them feel responsible for what happens in the gymnasium. Remember, even if you enlist your students to help create rules, it is your job to ensure that the rules are appropriate.

In addition to demonstrating and discussing rules, you need to post them in a prominent place in the gymnasium and provide pictures to convey the rules for nonreaders. Furthermore, you should inform parents and guardians of the rules as well as the consequences for violations. A good place to do so is in a beginning-of-school letter (see chapter 9 for an example).

For rules to be effective in the gymnasium, there must be consequences for breaking those rules. When discussing rules, make sure you go over the consequences and how they will be applied. More information about consequences will be presented later in the chapter.

Routines

Routines are procedures or protocols that happen daily in physical education. You should teach routines at the beginning of the school year. Routines provide structure and allow classes to run smoothly without delays, which leads to students spending more time in moderate to vigorous physical activity. Routines should be practiced by students, and students should be positively reinforced for performing routines correctly. Table 5.1 provides several classroom routines that are necessary for a physical education class to run efficiently.

Expectations

Expectations are what the teacher requires of each student. The main goal of setting classroom expectations is to help students understand what the teacher requires of them. Expectations should be high, and they should be communicated frequently at the beginning of the year, not just after students have failed to meet them (Rink, 2010). Research results have indicated that effective teachers articulate high, yet realistic, performance expectations for their students at the beginning of the year. Effective teachers make it clear that learning is the focus of the class; students are expected to master the curriculum and will be held accountable for their work (Brophy & Good, 1986).

You need to give some thought to the expectations that you will communicate to students at the beginning of the year. Common expectations in physical education include giving a good effort, being respectful, cooperating with others, and demonstrating good sporting behavior (Fink & Siedentop, 1989; O'Sullivan & Dyson, 1994).

▶ When students transition from one activity or location to another, should they walk single file or in pairs? Should they be allowed to talk during the transition?

Class Management Style

After establishing rules, routines, and expectations, you should develop an effective classroom management style. This style determines the level of success you will have in managing your class. Some teachers have a very efficient management style in which students move quickly and are held to high expectations in terms of completing management tasks. When teachers have an inefficient management style, the management tasks often take a great deal of time and detract from student learning and activity time.

To establish an efficient classroom management style, you should think about questions such as these: How quickly do I expect students to respond to my stop and go signals? How fast do I want students to move during transitions? How will I deal with students who refuse to participate? What will I do with students who do not handle equipment in an appropriate manner?

Coming up with answers to these questions will be instrumental in helping you develop a good managerial style. When planning a managerial style, you should also give thought to other practices such as starting the lesson in an effective manner and having good transitions that contribute to the efficiency of the managerial system.

TABLE 5.1

Classroom Routines

Routine	Sample description of routine
Entering the gymnasium	Walk in and begin the warm-up posted on the wall.
Leaving the gymnasium	Walk in a straight and orderly line.
Signal for stopping and starting	Voice commands: Go, freeze, stop Whistle Clap hands Hand in air
Getting drinks or going to the bathroom	Pass system: If a pass is available, a student may go to the bathroom or get a drink.
Distributing and collecting paperwork	Use squad leaders. Color-code paperwork for different classes.
Grouping students into pairs, small groups, and teams	Give students 5 seconds to find a partner or get into groups of a specific number. Use a deck of cards to group students by suit. Group by birthday months. Group by color of shirt.
Home base	Home base is where students always go to begin and end instruction: A specific line on the floor The center circle A box outlined on the floor
Handling equipment	Walk to obtain and put equipment away. Place equipment in a bin. Use specific students as equipment managers. Put equipment on the floor during instructions.
Locker room	Give a specific time limit and play music while students are changing. When the music stops, it serves as a 2-minute warning for students to be out of the locker room and in the gym.
Attendance	Attendance cards Group leader
Injuries	Everyone sits down. Teacher attends to injured student. Teacher sends two students for help if needed.
Emergency drills (fire, tornado, and so on)	Make sure students know what is expected during a drill or an actual emergency.

Starting Lessons

A lesson that begins well sets the tone for a successful class. Students tend to be more involved if a lesson begins quickly and there is little wait time. Be sure to start the class on time and have an entry routine that is active. Instead of having students enter the gym and sit in rows for attendance, have them enter the gym and begin a fitness activity or practice drill that is related to the unit and lesson objectives.

In addition to an active entry routine, you can use a time-saving routine for attendance. For example, students could enter the gym and place their attendance card in a specific place to show that they are present. Another example is to have students participate in their active entry routine in small groups and designate a group leader to report who is absent from the group.

Transitions

Learning to manage transitions is an essential skill for beginning physical education teachers. Tight transitions lead to reduced management time and more time for students to engage in activity. You need to state transitions clearly. One technique that I have found to be effective is to think of the transitions in a lesson as a transition sandwich. The first slice of bread in the sandwich is the "go" transition, and the other slice of bread is the "stop" transition. The activity that you want students to perform represents the meat in the middle of the two pieces of bread. The go transition begins with the phrase "When I say go . . ." and continues with the teacher explaining exactly what the students should do with equipment and where they should go to begin the activity. After the go transition, students perform the activity. The stop transition is signaled by a whistle blast or the word *stop* or *freeze*. The teacher then tells the students what to do next in terms of equipment and where to move for further instruction.

Another good idea is to set a time limit for the transition. For example, you could give the instructions for the transition as follows: "When I say go, you have 10 seconds to place your equipment in one of the three piles and come stand on the blue line. Ready, go. 10, 9, 8, 7 . . ."

Student Misbehavior

In addition to concerns about classroom management, you may have some reservations about your ability to address student misbehavior in an appropriate manner. Beginning teachers often think of discipline as punishment; however, discipline should not be synonymous with punishment. Discipline is about developing and maintaining appropriate behavior between teachers and their students and among students. For learning to take place, educational settings need high rates of appropriate behavior; furthermore, appropriate behavior is more than simply the absence of inappropriate behavior (Graham, Holt/Hale, & Parker, 2010).

You can do several things in order to become better prepared to deal with student misbehavior. Teacher behavior and actions can do a lot to promote and reinforce appropriate student behavior. Students tend to demonstrate more appropriate behavior when teachers have created a caring and supportive learning environment in which students feel important and feel physically and emotionally safe. On the other hand, negative teacher behaviors and student–teacher interactions can have a detrimental effect on the learning environment and student behavior. For example, you should avoid the following behaviors because they can diminish your effectiveness as a teacher:

▶ Being sarcastic
▶ Being confrontational
▶ Embarrassing students or making fun of them
▶ Losing your temper
▶ Being a pushover
▶ Making deals with students to obtain compliance

You need to understand that students who misbehave are often getting something from the misbehavior. For the most part, students do not choose to misbehave. They often make a bad decision, or there are circumstances that cause them to misbehave or to have trouble staying on task. Here are some common reasons why students misbehave:

▶ They want the teacher's attention.
▶ They are uncomfortable because of environmental issues (it is too hot or too cold in the PE area).
▶ They are upset about something that happened earlier or at home.
▶ They are embarrassed.
▶ They are tired.
▶ They don't feel well.
▶ They are trying to get the attention of their classmates.
▶ The skill they are practicing is too difficult or too easy.
▶ They do not like the activity or the curriculum.

You must try to understand why the misbehavior is occurring. Misbehaviors can often be addressed by understanding the reason a student is misbehaving, determining what a student is getting from the behavior, and taking steps to resolve the issue that is causing the misbehavior.

One way to gain insight into why a student is misbehaving is to have a conference with the student. Teacher–student conferences can be very helpful in curbing inappropriate behavior. These conferences also help you build a stronger relationship with students and allow you to let students know that you care about them as individuals. Here are some steps you should take when conducting a teacher–student conference regarding a student's misbehavior:

- ▶ Be courteous when greeting the student.
- ▶ Begin the meeting by stating that the purpose of the conference is to work together to resolve a problem.
- ▶ Listen to the student and take notes.
- ▶ When discussing the behavior with the student, make it clear that your problem is with the misbehavior, not with the student as a person.
- ▶ Be positive and firm with the student.
- ▶ Brainstorm some solutions with the student by asking questions such as these: What could you do differently? What will you do the next time something happens?
- ▶ Make a plan that is simple to carry out.

▶ If a student misbehaves during class, react calmly and courteously, and try to determine the reason for his or her actions.

Another approach to dealing with misbehavior is to replace inappropriate behaviors with behaviors that are more appropriate. One way to do this is to set up situations where students can demonstrate appropriate behaviors. As a teacher, you must always look for opportunities to catch the students being good. In addition, you should prompt the students to remind them about the expected behaviors. Reinforce appropriate behavior every time the students engage in it. You can do this by providing praise or a smile. Over time, you can diminish the reinforcement and just reinforce the behavior intermittently.

Classroom Management Plan

A good classroom management plan will ensure that the class runs efficiently and will provide you with a plan for dealing with student misbehavior. A classroom management plan has several components, including rules, routines, expectations, unacceptable student behaviors, proactive and reactive strategies, and negative consequences for student misbehavior. Resource 5.2 provides a template for creating a classroom management plan.

Part of a good classroom management plan is building good behavior in your students so that you can create a classroom atmosphere in which students respond to each other with respect and cooperation. Positive discipline can be developed by building relationships and a sense of community through teacher modeling, clear rules, routines, expectations, and consistency in dealing with students. Rules, routines, and expectations have been addressed earlier in this chapter; however, they are essential aspects of a classroom management plan.

Proactive and Reactive Strategies

Proactive strategies are techniques that a physical education teacher can use to increase the likelihood that appropriate behavior will continue (Graham, Holt/Hale, & Parker, 2010). For example, verbal and nonverbal interactions can be very effective for promoting appropriate behavior. Verbal interactions such as verbal praise and prompting students to do what is expected are effective techniques. Effective nonverbal interactions will communicate to students that you like the way they are behaving; techniques you may use include smiling, clapping, and giving a high five or a thumbs-up. Another strategy that works well with elementary children is to point out students who are behaving appropriately; for example, you might say, "I like the way John and Allison are listening and looking at me." Typically, this will prompt other elementary children to listen and look at the teacher; however, this method is not as effective with secondary students.

Reactive strategies are also used to increase appropriate behavior; however, these are used after inappropriate behavior has occurred (Graham, Holt/Hale, & Parker, 2010). For example, nonverbal teacher interactions such as using proximity control and making eye contact with a student are useful after an inappropriate behavior has occurred. Proximity control is achieved by moving close to the misbehaving student in order to reduce the behavior. In addition, you can use a signal such as bringing your finger to your mouth to signal that a student needs to be quiet or pointing at your eyes to signal that the student needs to pay attention.

Negative Consequences

Although proactive and reactive techniques are often effective in promoting appropriate student behavior, there are times when these strategies do not work and when students continue to misbehave. In this case, you will need to use other techniques to address the misbehavior. In the classroom management plan, these are referred to as negative consequences that are used when other techniques are ineffective. Consequences for unacceptable behaviors should be logical and appropriate. The purpose of using logical consequences is to motivate students to make responsible decisions, not to control students or force them to be submissive.

Students need to believe that you will enforce rules consistently and administer an appropriate consequence. You must be fair, but you should also realize that this might mean applying different consequences in different situations. For example, if a student repeatedly puts others down, the consequence for him or her would be different from that for a student who put another student down once. Make sure that students understand that fair and equal are not always the same. To be fair, you must ensure that your consequences are always reasonable and appropriate.

When giving consequences, you should have a friendly but firm tone of voice. You need to be respectful of the student and separate the student from the behavior. Communicate that you like the student as a person but that the student's behavior was inappropriate.

Although negative consequences are often used in physical education to discipline students for inappropriate behavior, you must be cautious when using negative consequences. Negative consequences can deter students from making inappropriate decisions, but these consequences will not necessarily turn students who behave poorly into well-behaved students. In addition, some students may not respond to negative consequences as a result of their home life. For these students, if a teacher gives them negative consequences, the students may view the teacher as another adult who treats them badly. In this case, the consequence will not be effective, and the students will continue to misbehave.

Various types of negative consequences may be used as part of your classroom management plan. Time-outs can be effective with elementary children; however, as students get older, they often want to get out of participating, and they welcome the opportunity to go to a time-out. In this instance, another technique may be more appropriate. For example, you could use a planning time-out. When given a planning time-out, the student must fill out a questionnaire that includes questions such as "What did you do that resulted in going to time-out?" and "What can you do next time to avoid going to time-out?" After responding to the questions in a timely manner, the student brings the planning sheet to the teacher, and the teacher has a short discussion with the student before letting the student continue to participate.

Another consequence is sending a student to a "buddy" teacher. A buddy teacher is another teacher in the building who is in close proximity to the gymnasium and will accept a misbehaving student from physical education into his or her class. The student will not participate in the buddy teacher's class; instead, the student will essentially be in a time-out while in the buddy teacher's classroom.

▶ Putting an elementary-school child in a time-out can be an effective negative consequence, but older students might require a different approach.

Contacting parents is another consequence. Typically, a phone call or note to parents will be effective in addressing inappropriate behavior, although sometimes you might need to request a parent–teacher conference. Chapter 9 includes some specific tips for contacting parents and conducting conferences.

A behavior contract is another consequence that a teacher can use to address specific issues. A behavior contract creates a formal agreement between you and the student. Behavior contracts define the problem, give specific actions that are expected of the student, and explain the rewards that students will receive for performing those actions. These rewards need to be important to students and should be given shortly after students have fulfilled the conditions of the contract. Resource 5.3 provides a template for creating a behavior contract. If a student continues to misbehave, the teacher can give detentions or referrals to an administrator.

Detentions

Teachers often use a detention as punishment; however, a detention should not be used to punish, but rather to resolve a problem with a student. When sending students to detention, you should provide them with activities that will address the problem they had in class that led to the detention. For example, during the detention, you could talk to the student about the problem and how it can be resolved. You could also ask students to write their thoughts about why they are serving the detention and what they can do to prevent the problem from happening again. In addition, you can ask them to write about some of their inappropriate behaviors and why it would benefit them to change their behavior.

One final note: Detentions should be used after a teacher has exhausted other options to curb misbehavior. You need to understand your district's policy on student detentions, as well as what you can do if a student refuses to serve the detention. In addition, it is a good idea to send the detention notice home so that parents are aware of the detention. Ask that parents sign and return the detention form to provide documentation that they know about the detention.

Referrals to an Administrator

You should not send students to administrators for minor misbehaviors that administrators expect you as the teacher to handle. Yet, when all else fails, you will need assistance from an administrator in dealing with a student whose misbehavior continues to negatively affect the learning environment. Certain behaviors are identified on the classroom management plan as unacceptable. These behaviors are considered unacceptable because they should result in the student being sent automatically to an administrator. Behaviors that should always be referred to an administrator include the following:

- Bullying
- Violent behavior
- Sexual harassment
- Bringing a weapon to school
- Persistent defiance
- Stealing
- Vandalism
- Substance abuse

Summary

As a beginning teacher, you may be apprehensive about your ability to manage a classroom, promote good student behavior, and address student misbehavior. You have several tools at your disposal to cultivate effective classroom management skills. These tools include developing a good classroom management plan that includes rules, routines, and expectations as well as proactive and reactive techniques for promoting good behavior. The classroom management plan also includes consequences you can use when proactive and reactive techniques have failed.

DISCUSSION QUESTIONS

1. What is a major point to remember when addressing the misbehavior of a student?

2. What are the components of a classroom management plan? How does this plan help you to be a more effective teacher?

3. What are negative consequences? Which consequences do you think are the most effective and why?

4. How would you explain to a student that fair and equal are not always the same when students are given consequences for misbehavior?

Discipline Log Template

Date	Student name	Inappropriate behavior	Response to inappropriate behavior	Follow-up actions

From A. James, 2013, *Survive and thrive as a physical educator: Strategies for the first year and beyond* (Champaign, IL: Human Kinetics).

Classroom Management Plan Template

Teacher: _____

1. Rules (classroom rules stated positively)

2. Routines

3. Expectations

4. Proactive behaviors (used to promote good behavior)

   a.

   b.

   c.

5. Nonverbal reactive techniques (used to stop inappropriate behavior and promote good behavior)

6. Verbal reactive techniques (used to stop inappropriate behavior and promote good behavior)

7. Negative consequences (used when reactive techniques do not work)

8. Behaviors that are unacceptable and will result in students being sent to an administrator

From A. James, 2013, *Survive and thrive as a physical educator: Strategies for the first year and beyond* (Champaign, IL: Human Kinetics).

Behavior Contract Template

This behavior contract is between _____ (student) and _____ (teacher). The contract is being put in place to address a specific issue that has been occurring in physical education.

Describe problem below.

_____

_____

_____

_____

The following actions are required of _____ (student) to meet the terms of this contract.

_____

_____

_____

_____

If these actions are achieved by _____ (date),

_____ (student) will be entitled to the following reward.

_____

_____

_____

_____

_____	_____	_____	_____
Student's signature	Date	Teacher's signature	Date

_____   _____
Third party signature   Date

From A. James, 2013, *Survive and thrive as a physical educator: Strategies for the first year and beyond* (Champaign, IL: Human Kinetics).

PART II

Skills
to Help
You Thrive

CHAPTER 6

Motivating Students

Motivating students to participate in physical education can be an overwhelming task. Student motivation is often a problem for beginning and experienced teachers alike. The good news is that there are specific actions and techniques that you can use to motivate students to participate, improve their skills, and demonstrate good sporting behavior. This chapter discusses various types of motivation and provides examples of how they are manifested by students in physical education classes. In addition, the chapter covers techniques that can be used to motivate students and enhance student learning.

Types of Motivation

There are three types of motivation: intrinsic motivation, extrinsic motivation, and amotivation. All three types of motivation can be observed in physical education. To enhance the teaching-learning process in physical education, you must understand the three types of motivation as well as the techniques that can be used to address each type.

In physical education, some students are motivated because they enjoy participating in physical activity and learning new skills. These students are intrinsically motivated to participate. Individuals who are intrinsically motivated will seek out challenges to explore, learn, and master a task or activity (Ryan & Deci, 2000).

Research results have indicated that students who are intrinsically motivated pay more attention to teachers and concentrate on the tasks at hand. In addition, they do not feel guilty, pressured, or bored when participating in physical education (Ntoumanis, 2005). Research has also shown that students who possess intrinsic motivation in physical education often intend to participate in optional physical education courses the following year; these students are also more likely to plan on being physically active after leaving school (Ntoumanis, 2001, 2005). These results are important because one of the goals of physical education teachers is to help ensure that students value physical activity and that they continue to be active outside of school hours and after they graduate.

In physical education, you can help students develop intrinsic motivation by providing positive experiences that promote cooperative learning and emphasize individual improvement (Ntoumanis, 2001). Personal improvement can be emphasized by avoiding making comparisons between students and by encouraging students to practice and compare their current performance to past performances.

In contrast to intrinsic motivation, extrinsic motivation is when a student performs a task or behavior in order to receive some outcome separate from the activity; the outcome is valued more than the activity itself (Ntoumanis, 2005; Ryan & Deci, 2000). Four types of extrinsic motivation have been identified: external regulation, introjected regulation, identified regulation, and integrated regulation (Ryan & Deci, 2000). External regulation represents behaviors that are regulated through external means, such as rewards or punishment (Ntoumanis, 2001, 2005; Ryan & Deci, 2000).

External rewards are commonly used in physical education. For example, when I taught at the elementary level, my school used "funny" money as an external reward. Students could earn funny money in any class, and they were able to save money to be used at a carnival at the end of the school year. As a teacher, I rewarded students with funny money for putting forth effort to improve, for participation, and for good sporting behavior. This extrinsic reward was very popular with students; however, as students got older, I gave less and less funny money in an effort to decrease the extrinsic reward provided by the money.

Other common rewards used in physical education include earning points for specific behaviors, earning free time or "choice" days, and being recognized on posters or bulletin boards. For example, I had a bulletin board that was dedicated to students who were "on the ball." I would reward students for skill performance, effort, and sporting behavior by putting their names on cutouts of various types of balls on the bulletin board.

Another extrinsic reward that I implemented was the Sport of the Month Award and the Classroom Sport of the Month Award. My elementary school held an assembly every month. At this assembly, a boy and a girl would be chosen as the Sport of the Month for their class, and they would receive a certificate. Resource 6.1 provides an example of a Sport of the Month certificate. The Classroom Sport of the Month award was awarded to the classroom that as a whole demonstrated the best sporting behavior. The classroom that won the Sport of the Month Award received a large trophy that was housed in their classroom for the month.

These rewards worked well to motivate students to demonstrate good sporting behavior; however, I question whether the students' sporting behavior would have continued had I withdrawn these rewards. Although some of my students may have been intrinsically motivated to demonstrate good sporting behavior, others may not have been motivated to do so without the incentive of the reward.

One concern about using external rewards such as these is that the reward may decrease the intrinsic motivation of some students. This may occur if students perceive that the reward is given in order to control their behavior. In addition, if students with high levels of intrinsic motivation fail to receive a reward, this may cause them to believe that they are not competent in their sporting behavior. As a result, their intrinsic motivation to demonstrate good sporting behavior may be decreased.

Amotivation is another type of motivation that unfortunately is very common in physical education, particularly at the secondary level. Amotivated behavior occurs in situations where individuals are neither intrinsically nor extrinsically motivated (Ntoumanis, 2001). Students who are amotivated do not act at all, or they act without intent and just go through the motions (Ryan & Deci, 2000). Research results show that students who lack physical competence usually find physical education meaningless (amotivation) as well as boring (Ntoumanis, 2001; Ntoumanis, Pensgaard, Martin, & Pipe, 2004). These results emphasize the importance of physical educators helping all students develop competence in physical activities at an early age. By doing this, physical educators can enhance students' motivation to participate in physical activity throughout their lifespan, which decreases the chances of students leading a sedentary life.

Techniques for Motivating Students

When it comes to motivating students to participate and develop skills and knowledge in physical education, there are several things you can do. One idea is to create and foster good student–teacher relationships. The benefits of developing relationships with students are far reaching; however, one of the most compelling benefits is that if students like and respect you as a teacher, they will be more motivated to participate in physical education.

Earning Students' Respect

"Respect begets respect" is a saying that teachers need to embrace. As a teacher, you must earn the respect of your students. Even with the best planned lessons, if you have not earned your students' respect, you will not be successful in motivating your students. Earning students' respect can be difficult at all levels, but it can be particularly tricky for new teachers at the secondary level because they are often close in age to their students.

You can earn the respect of your students through daily interactions. Students respect teachers who are fair, consistent, prepared, and concerned about them as individuals as well as about their learning in physical education. Beginning teachers often make the mistake of being a "buddy" to students instead of being the adult in charge of the class. They believe that students will respect them if they are a buddy. This approach often backfires. When the teacher tries to address problems that arise, students become upset because they did not see their relationship with the teacher as a teacher–student relationship.

Even if you gain the respect of your students, you must be careful not to lose that respect. Several teacher behaviors can cause students to lose respect for a teacher:

▶ Rolling out the ball for games that do not require planning (shows a lack of preparation)

▶ Losing your temper

▶ Treating students unfairly

▶ Failing to be a good role model who displays appropriate behaviors

▶ Being sarcastic and uncaring toward students

▶ Not listening to students

▶ Not knowing or being able to perform the content of physical education

Developing Good Teacher–Student Relationships

One way to develop relationships with students is to be available and visible to them. Many relationships with students begin in the classroom but are nurtured through interactions in the cafeteria and hallway. Be sure to acknowledge students by name and offer a smile or encouragement. In this way, students know that you really care about them and that they can approach you with any of their concerns.

Students will regularly come to see you at lunch or before and after school. Some students will just want to spend some time with you, but many will seek you out when something is bothering them. Make sure you listen to students, but be careful about giving advice. You want the students to trust you and to believe that you will listen, offer support, and encourage them to make a good decision. In some situations, you may need to make a referral to the school counselor in order to provide the support that the student needs.

Another way to connect with students is to find out what matters most to them. To be an effective teacher, you need to develop an understanding of what is important to your students. You should try to develop insight into areas such as speech patterns (slang), music, movie and television preferences, popular celebrities, newsworthy stories, and styles of dress. Although gaining insight into the social culture of students is essential, you should not become immersed in that culture. Problems can arise in the classroom when students believe that the characteristics of the teacher's culture are the same as theirs.

▶ One way to motivate students is to talk to them about their concerns and show that you are available and interested in their perspective.

Finally, students will be curious about you as a person and will eventually ask you personal questions. How you respond to these questions is up to you; however, you need to share part of yourself with your students in order to develop relationships with them. You must give some thought to what information you will share with students. Students will often ask questions about your family, what you do in your free time, where you live, and so on. If you are uncomfortable answering these questions, the best strategy is to have a response planned that will satisfy student interest while only providing information within the parameters that you are comfortable with. For example, you may not be comfortable telling students where you live; in this case, you can respond with a town or city rather than an exact address. If you are not comfortable responding to questions about your family or living situation, you can respond to students in a manner that is vague rather than give specific details. For example, you may refer to stepchildren as your children rather than go into details regarding your marriage or primary relationship that resulted in the stepchildren becoming part of your family. The following list provides some tips for connecting with students.

▶ Learn students' names and use them.

▶ Project a caring attitude toward all students.

▶ Treat all students equitably.

▶ Stress things that you and your students have in common.

▶ Use good manners when you deal with students and compliment them when they do the same.

▶ Be generous with your praise.

▶ Listen carefully and pay attention to students' body language.

▶ Try not to interrupt the student and avoid distractions such as telephone calls when speaking with students.

▶ Do not judge students.

▶ Refrain from giving advice. Encourage the student to make good decisions.

▶ On occasion, repeat what the student has told you by saying, "If I understand you, this is what you are saying . . ."

▶ Follow up with students and check in with them in regard to how they are doing on a regular basis.

▶ Attend student events—such as athletic contests, musical recitals, and art shows—where students are able to display their talents.

Using Instructional Techniques to Motivate Students

In addition to earning students' respect and developing positive relationships with students, you can also use specific instructional techniques that are effective in motivating students. According to Brophy and Kher (1986), four conditions need to be created in order to motivate students to learn, and teachers can create these conditions by doing the following:

1. Present tasks that are developmentally appropriate.

2. Present tasks that have meaning to students and contribute toward learning objectives.

3. Present a variety of tasks to minimize boredom.

4. Present tasks as learning opportunities, and provide students with assistance and encouragement to help them accomplish the tasks.

Present Tasks That Are Developmentally Appropriate Activities that are developmentally appropriate contribute to students' intrinsic motivation to participate. Developmentally appropriate tasks motivate students because the tasks are challenging and not too easy or too difficult. If a task is too simple or too difficult, it will likely reduce student motivation to continue participating.

Teaching by invitation and intratask variation are two ways to ensure developmental appropriateness and to motivate students who are at different skill levels. Teaching by invitation is when you invite the whole class to change the task in some way; however, some students may choose to not change the task (Graham, Holt/Hale, & Parker, 2010). For example, you may state the following: "At this time if you are comfortable throwing the ball at the target from your spot, I invite you to make it more difficult by moving back two giant steps. If you believe you need more practice from your current spot, you are welcome to stay at that spot."

Intratask variation involves changing the task for an individual student or a small group of students (Graham, Holt/Hale, & Parker, 2010). This is useful when a task is appropriate for most students but a single student or a small group of students are either struggling with the task or finding it too easy. In this situation, to motivate students to stay on task and keep learning, you should have a conversation with the individual student or small group and change the task as needed for them while the other students continue to practice the original task.

Present Tasks That Have Meaning and Contribute Toward Learning Objectives Students should find learning tasks meaningful, and the tasks should meet students' personal interests. As a teacher, you need to find ways to present tasks that have meaning and importance to students. At the same time, you must ensure that students are working to accomplish learning objectives through these tasks.

One way to do this is to plan the physical education curriculum in a manner that offers students choices of activities. Many physical education teachers use an activity interest survey to determine students' interests and then plan their curricular offerings based on the results. The survey could also include questions about why the students participate in physical activity. For example, are students physically active because they want to enhance their physical fitness, because they want to be with their friends and have fun, or because they want to improve their appearance? Students have various reasons for choosing to participate in physical activity. It is your job to determine their reasons and needs for participation and to provide activities that allow them to meet their needs. Resource 6.2 provides an example of an activity interest survey that a teacher could use when making decisions about curricular offerings.

Curriculum models are used to deliver tasks in a meaningful way that also contributes to learning outcomes. Curriculum models focus on specific, relevant, and challenging outcomes that allocate more time for learners to be engaged with learning (Lund & Tannehill, 2010). Some of the common curriculum models include Sport Education, Adventure Education, and the Skill Theme Approach.

The goal of Sport Education is to develop competent, literate, and enthusiastic sportspersons (Siedentop, Hastie, & van der Mars, 2011). The model has several features that mimic authentic sport experiences, such as seasons, affiliation, formal competition, record keeping, and culminating events. In addition, this model includes an emphasis on fair play and developing game sense. Game sense is a combination of learning skills, applying tactics, and understanding rules (Siedentop, Hastie, & van der Mars, 2011). Furthermore, students take on different

▶ In the Adventure Education curriculum model, students can choose to try activities, such as climbing, that present different forms of challenges and risks.

roles in the model, such as player roles, team roles (i.e., coach, trainer), duty team roles (i.e., official, scorekeeper), and specialist roles (i.e., line judge in volleyball).

Adventure Education is a model that focuses on the development of interpersonal and intrapersonal relationships through the use of activities that involve challenges and an uncertainty of the final outcome (Lund & Tannehill, 2010). Adventure Education involves the practice of group processing (debriefing) of learning activities. Debriefing helps students sort information in a meaningful way, and it allows them to focus on issues arising from the experience and to verbally reflect on and analyze the experience (Lund & Tannehill, 2010).

Another feature of Adventure Education is the concept of challenge by choice. Challenge by choice implies that students can choose from a variety of activities with different levels of physical and emotional challenges that involve a degree of risk. The final aspect of Adventure Education is the full value contract. The full value contract is a social contract that group members agree to adhere to in regard to personal behavior and group interactions.

The Skill Theme Approach is a model that is commonly used at the elementary level. The approach is built around skill themes and movement concepts. Skill themes are the fundamental movements that build the foundation for sports and physical activities, such as throwing, kicking, and striking. Movement concepts enhance the quality of a movement. For example, the skill theme of throwing can be enhanced by the movement concept of force, such as throwing the ball hard at the wall.

The Skill Theme Approach has four characteristics. The first is that students will develop competence in performing a variety of locomotor, nonmanipulative, and manipulative motor skills. Second, the approach is designed to provide experiences that are appropriate to a child's developmental level, as opposed to age or grade level. Third, the scope and sequence of the skill themes are designed to reflect the varying needs and interests of students over a period of years. Finally, the approach emphasizes instructional alignment, which involves the teacher deciding on objectives for a lesson, developing a series of tasks to accomplish the objectives, and designing assessments to determine if the lesson objectives have been achieved (Graham, Holt/Hale, & Parker, 2010).

These three curriculum models are very popular, but other models are also available that enable teachers to present tasks in a meaningful manner while helping students achieve learning objectives. Figure 6.1 provides several resources for more information about curriculum models.

Present a Variety of Tasks to Minimize Boredom   Another way to motivate students is to offer a variety of tasks. Teachers should use

Bulger, S.M., Mohr, D.J., Rairigh, R.M., & Townsend, J.S. (2006). *Sport education seasons: Featuring basketball, soccer and fitness education.* Champaign, IL: Human Kinetics.

Lund, J., & Tannehill, D. (2010). *Standards-based physical education curriculum development* (2nd ed.). Sudbury, MA: Jones and Bartlett Publishers.

Metzler, M.W. (2005). *Instructional models for physical education* (2nd ed.). Scottsdale, AZ: Holcomb Hathaway Publishers.

Mitchell, S.A., Oslin, J.L., & Griffin, L.L. (2006). *Teaching sport concepts and skills: A tactical games approach* (2nd ed.). Champaign, IL: Human Kinetics.

Siedentop, D., Hastie, P.A., & van der Mars, H. (2011). *Complete guide to sport education* (2nd ed.). Champaign, IL: Human Kinetics.

▶ **FIGURE 6.1** Resources for information on curriculum models.

a variety of interesting tasks that will maintain student engagement and motivate students to practice. By creating lessons and units that have strong content development (as discussed in chapter 3), you will motivate students to participate and learn in physical education.

In addition, students are motivated if they are working on a task that is conducted in an authentic situation. For example, performing tasks in the context of the game is more authentic—and thus more motivating—than performing a task against a wall or in a circle.

Students are also motivated when tasks are challenging but allow for some level of success; the tasks should also be designed to enhance the students' level of competence in performing the task. Physical education teachers can use several instructional techniques to help ensure student success.

- ▶ **Use self-adjusting activities.** In these activities, students can choose to adjust the activity in order to make it more challenging or to allow them to be more successful. For example, you may give students the option of moving closer to a target or moving farther away based on their ability.

- ▶ **Use self-testing activities.** Tasks that challenge students to test their abilities are very motivating. For example, a task could involve partners seeing how many times they can throw the ball back and forth without missing. This type of task can engage students as well as maintain their motivation.

▶ **Change the height of the goal or target.** Adjust the height of the goal or target so students can be successful.

▶ **Change the width of the goal.** Make the goal wider or more narrow depending on the skill level of the students.

▶ **Change court dimensions.** Make the court wide, narrow, long, or short.

▶ **Change to secondary rules.** If a rule (such as traveling in basketball) destroys the continuous nature of play, you may consider modifying that rule.

▶ **Change equipment.** Make sure that equipment is developmentally appropriate. Changing the type or size of equipment to make it easier to control can help ensure success.

Another way to motivate students and add variety to tasks is to use technology in physical education. Physical educators have a variety of technology at their disposal to use in instruction. For example, heart rate monitors and pedometers can be very motivating to students. You can use heart rate monitors to teach students about the importance of intensity and its connection to enhancing cardiovascular fitness.

Pedometers are tools that can help teach the importance of physical activity and can motivate students to set goals related to being more physically active. For example, students could wear pedometers during physical education classes and record the steps taken during various activities. Students could then graph the steps they took in those activities to identify which activities caused them to be more active. This will help students make informed activity choices.

Present Tasks as Learning Opportunities for Students and Provide Assistance and Encouragement Teachers must present tasks as opportunities for students to learn and improve. Although students may fear that they cannot perform a task perfectly, most will work to improve their skills. As a teacher, you should assist students in their performance of skills and help them attribute their improvement and successes to their effort and practice. You can also help students enhance their performance by giving them explicit criteria for performance and providing appropriate feedback to improve their performance. In addition, effective praise provides information to students about their competence or the value of their accomplishments; praise should also attribute success to effort and ability, which implies to students that they will be successful in the future (Brophy & Good, 1986). You should use verbal and nonverbal praise to communicate

TABLE 6.1

Verbal and Nonverbal Praise

Verbal praise	Nonverbal praise
Tricia, you are really good at keeping your body in a tucked position while you are rolling.	Thumbs-up
Juan, I really liked the way you helped Demetrius today with his layup shot.	High five
Maya, you are much better at shooting because you are keeping your elbow in on the shot.	Clapping hands

with students about their performance in addition to encouraging them to continue to participate. Table 6.1 provides examples of various types of verbal and nonverbal praise that you can use to motivate students.

Note that there are some specific guidelines for providing praise. First, you must make it honest and credible. Second, you should individualize praise that you give to students. To do this, you must know your students and must be sensitive to the manner in which they respond to praise. For example, some students may not respond positively to praise given in public; however, they may respond well to praise given in private. Finally, you should make praise specific rather than general so that students believe that their effort and progress are important to you as the teacher (Rink, 2010).

Summary

Motivating students in physical education can be a difficult task. You must use instructional techniques that help students develop intrinsic motivation to participate in physical activity. In addition, you can use other techniques such as earning students' respect and developing positive teacher–student relationships in order to motivate students to partake in physical activity and physical education class.

Finally, you must be aware of strategies that motivate students to learn, such as presenting developmentally appropriate tasks that are meaningful and contribute toward learning objectives. In addition, students are motivated when teachers present a variety of tasks as well as tasks that are presented as learning opportunities combined with assistance and encouragement from the teacher.

DISCUSSION QUESTIONS

1. Why is it important to foster and help develop intrinsic motivation in students?

2. What are some techniques that can be used to motivate students to participate and learn in physical education?

3. Why is developing positive relationships with students important in regard to motivating students to participate in physical education?

4. What specifically can you do to promote positive relationships with students?

SPORT OF THE MONTH AWARD

This certificate is awarded to

· ·

for being the Sport of the Month for _____

in _____ 's class.

This certificate is awarded to recognize _____

for outstanding sporting behavior in physical education.

From A. James, 2013, *Survive and thrive as a physical educator: Strategies for the first year and beyond* (Champaign, IL: Human Kinetics).

Sample Activity Interest Survey

Name: _____ Date: _____

Grade level: _____

Directions: For each activity below, indicate your interest by placing an X under your level of interest. If you have a strong interest in the activity, place an X under "Strong interest." If you have an interest in the activity, but it is not a strong interest, place an X under "Interest." If you have little interest in the activity, place an X under "Little interest." Only mark one column per activity.

Activity	Strong interest	Interest	Little interest
Archery			
Basketball			
Dance			
Field hockey			
Floor hockey			
Golf			
Ice skating			
Lacrosse			
Mountain biking			
Orienteering			
Pickleball			
Rock wall			
Snowboarding			

Are there activities that you are interested in that are not on the list?

Why do you participate in physical activity?

CHAPTER 7

Diversity in Physical Education

One of the most daunting tasks that you face is learning how to work with students from diverse backgrounds. Diversity has several aspects, including culture, race, gender, religion, disability, sexual orientation, and social class. In writing this chapter, I recognized that it would be impossible to fully address all aspects of diversity and cover how they relate to physical education. In light of this, I decided to focus on culture, disability, gender, and sexual orientation.

Several factors influenced my decision to concentrate on these areas of diversity. First, when I was a beginning teacher, my knowledge of these topics was not strong. In fact, my understanding of other cultures, gender issues, and issues about sexual orientation in respect to teaching physical education was almost nonexistent. My awareness of students with disabilities was minimal, and the knowledge that I had was acquired from one university class. Second, as a teacher educator, I am aware that preservice physical education teachers today do not have a strong knowledge base regarding diversity and how to enhance the learning environment for diverse learners. Third, many of my previous students who have secured teaching jobs have expressed to me the frustration of not understanding different cultures. They have also told me that their lack of understanding has left them unsure in some situations when teaching diverse learners. Finally, the goal of this chapter is not to provide a comprehensive description of diversity, but to provide a basic level of knowledge that will benefit beginning physical education teachers.

Stereotypes

Several events have occurred in the world recently that illustrate the lack of understanding that individuals have about different cultures and groups of people. For example, September 11, 2001, will always be remembered as a day of horror and destruction in the United States. The attack on the twin towers was the impetus for wars in Iraq and Afghanistan, as well as a precursor to a great deal of anti–Middle Eastern sentiment in the United States.

Where were you on September 11, 2001? What do you remember? Do you think that cultural differences may have played a role in the attack? I was a doctoral student at the University of Massachusetts and happened to be teaching a diversity class. Students in my class had diverse ethnic backgrounds and represented a variety of countries, including Pakistan, Iran, China, Vietnam, and the United States. They represented different racial and ethnic groups, religions, genders, and sexual orientations. We had been in class for a short time, and the students were just beginning to learn about diversity in terms of what made them and their classmates unique; however, when we had class on September 12, 2001, the day after the attack, the discussion that ensued was perhaps one of the best learning experiences that I have had the privilege to take part in.

At first, students did not really want to discuss the incident, but I saw it as a teachable moment and began to talk about my understanding of this catastrophic event. As I presented my perspective, students began to speak up, and we discussed several issues, including how the West is perceived by the Middle East. My students from Pakistan shared that they were afraid to go to class after the attack for fear of harassment or even physical violence. We tried to make sense of the attack and to understand the role that culture and religion may have played. The conversation was fascinating, and the discussion brought to light a great deal about how cultural misunderstandings and stereotypes can affect not only individuals and religious groups but also entire countries.

Even today, as a result of the September 11th attack (as well as other terrorist attacks) and misunderstandings about the Muslim community, incidents of harassment continue to occur toward Muslims or other people who may be perceived as Muslim because of their appearance and physical characteristics. This is unfortunate and in part has resulted from the idea that Muslims are equated with violence, an image that misrepresents many Muslims who are successful, educated, and non-violent (Nydell, 1996). Furthermore, Pew Forum on Religion and Public Life (2011) reported that most Muslim Americans are middle class and mainstream.

This example illustrates how certain groups are portrayed and often stereotyped in the media and in general. People often make assumptions about individuals who belong to different racial or ethnic groups based on stereotypes that are erroneous or gross overgeneralizations. Stereotypes exist about many cultural groups. For example, Asian Americans are known as the "model minority." They have been depicted as hardworking, quiet, intelligent, and academically talented. The problem is that not all Asian Americans are model students. Not all are bright or even speak English (Schuman, 2004). When teachers walk into a classroom and see an Asian American face, they often assume that the student is academically able and well behaved. This stereotype, however, often harms students because they may not get the academic and behavioral support they need.

Stereotypes are perceptions, and those perceptions often become reality. The beliefs that teachers hold about stereotypes of different cultural groups also affect how they interact and teach diverse learners. I was discussing stereotypes in one of my college classes, and I asked students to tell me the first thing they thought of when I named a racial or ethnic group. For example, I specified Asian Americans, and my students responded, "Smart." I specified African Americans, and the students responded, "Good athletes." Their perceptions of these groups were clouded by stereotypes. Obviously, if beginning teachers do not examine these stereotypes and see the danger of believing false stereotypes, their instruction and relationships with students belonging to these racial and ethnic groups will suffer.

Some racial and ethnic groups fall victim to stereotypes that affect the success that students with these cultural backgrounds experience in school. For example, African American students who study hard and make good grades are often stereotyped within their own community as "acting white." Very often this stereotype as well as peer pressure leads African American students to not place a high value on academic success (Davis, 2007). Be sure to note that this is just a stereotype—many African American students do not fall victim to this stereotype, and they experience great academic success in school.

The number of people who believe these stereotypes may surprise you. As an educator, if you make educational decisions in regard to instruction, classroom management, and assessment based on stereotypes, this will lead to stereotyped students experiencing a level of inequality in the gymnasium. In the end, these stereotypes often become self-fulfilling prophecies, and students may behave and achieve in a manner that aligns with the educator's stereotyped expectations.

Understanding Diversity

As a beginning teacher in an urban area, I struggled with understanding my students and how our differences affected our interactions as well as our perceptions of each other in the gymnasium. It was only through the experience of teaching and working with diverse learners that I realized I had to understand my own diversity in order to appreciate the diversity of my students.

As a beginning physical education teacher, you need to examine your personal diversity and your beliefs regarding common stereotypes that may obscure your perceptions of different cultural groups. You must understand your own identity. Where did your family originate? What are some of your family traditions? Are some of these traditions based on religion or ethnicity? How does the culture you grew up in affect the way you view schools and teachers? How does your background influence how you view individuals from backgrounds different from your own? How does the color of your skin or the language you speak influence how others view you as an individual? Through asking yourself these questions, not only will you become more attuned to your identity, but you will also recognize any bias that you may have toward other groups. Once you become aware of any bias you may possess, you can examine how this bias could be influencing assumptions you may be making about individuals who belong to different groups. Resources 7.1 and 7.2 will help you reflect on your identity as well as the identities of your students. In addition, these resources will enable you to reflect on how your background influences your interactions with students and how their background influences how they interact with you as their teacher.

After you begin to understand who you are as an individual, you should attempt to understand your students' cultural backgrounds, including how their culture affects their view of physical education in general. You also need to learn how their culture affects the way they respond to you as the teacher. The next step in the process of examining diversity is to explore what culture is, as well as the cultural characteristics of various cultures. Note that this is a complex issue and that this text provides only basic information on cultural

▶ Coming from different cultural backgrounds can affect the way in which students interact with each other in physical education class and how they perceive the role of the teacher.

characteristics. You can use this information as a basis for understanding and then further investigate other areas of diversity and cultural characteristics.

Culture

Culture is a social system that represents an accumulation of beliefs, attitudes, habits, values, and practices that serve as a filter through which a group of people view and respond to the world in which they live (Shade, Kelly, & Oberg, 1997). Culture influences students in the gymnasium because they do not come to us as blank slates. They bring their own ideas and ways of viewing the world, which are shaped by their culture. Even veteran physical education teachers can have difficulty being effective when their culture differs from the culture of their students. For example, I taught for several years in an urban school with a student population that was primarily African American. Early in my teaching career, I was trying to speak to a young African American student about an incident in which his behavior was inappropriate. The student would not look at me while I was speaking, which was frustrating because I had been taught to look at an adult who was speaking to me. After I spoke with the student and sent him on his way, I spoke with an African American colleague about the incident. She explained to me that in the African American culture it is a sign of respect not to look an adult in the eye when that adult is disciplining the child. This experience made me begin to question my own cultural background and how it influenced my effectiveness as a physical education teacher of students who had very different cultural backgrounds than mine.

Race and ethnicity are aspects of culture. Race is defined as large groups of people distinguished from one another by their physical appearances (Lindsey, Robins, & Terrell, 2003). Race is a tough topic for educators to discuss for several reasons. For instance, as a white teacher of European descent, I was taught not to talk about race, ethnicity, or cultural differences. From early in life, I was taught to treat people the same way regardless of their race or ethnicity. I know from experience that several of my white colleagues had similar experiences. As a result, I have heard many teachers say, "I don't see skin color or gender. I only see my students." Thinking in this way can be counterproductive in the gymnasium because teachers do not embrace aspects of diversity (such as race and gender) that make people different. In addition, this way of thinking causes teachers to view those aspects of diversity as being a weakness instead of a strength that will enhance the teaching-learning environment. If teachers think in this way, they are doing students a disservice by choosing to ignore characteristics and experiences that define who the students are. When a teacher thinks of all students as the same, the teacher may also fail to recognize aspects of the students' diversity and how their diversity influences the teacher's interactions with students.

Ethnicity is not always distinguishable from race. Ethnicity includes not only genetic makeup but also behavior patterns, values, and religious perspectives. Ethnicity describes groups of people with a shared history, ancestry, geographic and linguistic origin, and physical type. Although ethnicity may be correlated with race, there may also be multiple ethnicities within a racial category (Lindsey, Robins, & Terrell, 2003).

People who share the same ethnicity, religion, and language or live in the same geographical areas develop a common way of interacting and thinking. Students' ideas about the world, their beliefs about and preferences for physical activity, and even their beliefs about acceptable behavior in school are shaped by their culture.

The following sections present several generalized characteristics that describe individual cultures in regard to family, language and communication patterns, and education. Although other characteristics exist, I chose these categories because of the significance they play in my understanding of and experiences in teaching diverse learners. In addition, they provide an overview of how the characteristics of different cultural groups vary. I recommend that you investigate other cultures and their characteristics in order to better understand cultures that might not be represented in this chapter. Although you must avoid stereotyping or prejudging a group, you need to have some understanding of generalized cultural characteristics in order to individualize instruction and meet the needs of your learners regardless of their cultural background. Again, remember that not all individuals belonging to these groups will exhibit the characteristics described.

Characteristics of Anglo-American Culture

Early in American history, the United States had a shared set of values and traditions that made up the Anglo-American culture. Many early American settlers emigrated from Northern European countries. The United States today has many immigrants and descendants of immigrants from countries of non-European origin. For people of Northern European descent, their way of life, thinking, and religion have been heavily influenced by Anglo-Saxon culture and their European backgrounds (Banks, 1997). Again, it is important to note that the following selected characteristics are generalizations and that many Anglo-Americans may not demonstrate these characteristics or may demonstrate variations of them.

Most Anglo-Americans value the family. In the Anglo-American family, sons and daughters are valued equally. The typical Anglo-American family includes the immediate family; a high priority is often not placed on the extended family. Although the family has a place of importance, Anglo-American adolescents place their peers in a higher position than their family (Baruth & Manning, 1992). In addition, Anglo-American adolescents tend to value their own individual desires more than the welfare of their family (Baruth & Manning, 1992).

In Anglo-American culture, verbal skills are highly valued. Anglo-Americans tend to be talkative and outgoing. The communication patterns of Anglo-Americans consist of speaking loudly and quickly. They tend to address listeners directly and often by name, and they tend to interrupt frequently. When communicating, individuals often avoid close physical contact and keep their distance. In addition, they tend to require lots of background information when interacting with others, such as information about what individuals do, their families, and where they live (Baruth & Manning, 1992; Shade, Kelly, & Oberg, 1997; Sinagatullin, 2003).

Anglo-Americans believe that education is important because it provides knowledge and develops attitudes that people need in order to become good citizens. In addition, education often leads to employment and well-paying careers (Sinagatullin, 2003).

Characteristics of Hispanic Culture

The Hispanic population consists of ethnically diverse communities, such as Mexicans, Cubans, Puerto Ricans, and others. Hispanics share a common language and some cultural values. The cultural heritage of Mexican Americans is mainly Native American but is heavily Spanish in language, religion, and customs. Puerto Ricans represent a blend of Native American, Spanish, and African heritages. Cuban Americans are generally descendants of former political refugees from Cuba (Sinagatullin, 2003). Although there are common characteristics among Hispanic Americans, they are a very diverse group and include subcultures that differ in customs, values, and educational orientation. Once again, it is important to note that the following cultural characteristics may not be representative of all Hispanics.

Family, community, and ethnic group are the main priorities for Hispanics. The extended family plays an important role in Hispanic culture. Males in the family are in a position of respect and authority. The role of women is somewhat subordinate to men. Typically, fathers have the most prestige and authority. Sons have more and earlier independence than daughters (Baruth & Manning, 2009).

Status and role definitions in the community and family are very clearly defined and should be respected. Male roles are closely associated with the concept of power, whereas roles of women are closely associated with traits of love, belonging, and religion (Sinagatullin, 2003). The role of males in Puerto Rican culture is influenced greatly by "machismo," which influences the behavior and attitudes of adolescent males. Machismo refers to the male's manhood, the courage to fight, and the manly traits of honor and dignity, which include keeping one's word and protecting one's name. It suggests a clear-cut distinction between the sexes whereby males can enjoy rights and privileges denied to women (Baruth & Manning, 2009).

Many varieties of Spanish are spoken among the Hispanic people in the United States. These varieties depend on where the speakers live, how long they have been in the United States, and where they originally came from. Although English may not be the primary language spoken by Hispanic individuals, they often understand English better than they speak it. When communicating, Hispanics will nod affirmatively; however, this may not necessarily mean agreement. Silence may signify a failure to understand and embarrassment about asking the speaker to repeat or clarify (Baruth & Manning, 2009; Shade, Kelly, & Oberg, 1997).

When teaching Hispanic students, you should be aware of several implications. First, these students are typically kinesthetic learners in that they need movement to become engaged in learning. Second, many Hispanics, particularly if not raised in the United States, may avoid eye contact with authority figures or in awkward situations. Third, you should use visual aids with demonstrations and should communicate in a clear and concise manner in order to help students who are English language learners. Fourth, it is helpful to use peer helpers when language difficulties are present. Finally, you should be careful when encouraging learners to excel above others in class because this goes against Hispanic cultural traditions and expectations (Culp, 2009).

Characteristics of African American Culture

African Americans are drawn from a diverse range of cultures and countries in Africa, the Caribbean, and Central and South America. Considerable diversity characterizes African American learners based on differences between lower, middle, and higher socioeconomic groups; between African Americans living in different geographic locations of the United States; and between urban and rural African Americans (Baruth & Manning, 2009).

Although cultural characteristics must be presented cautiously, some cultural generalizations exist irrespective of geographical location and socioeconomic status. However, these cultural generalizations may not be representative of all African Americans. For example, family is very important in the African American culture. African American children and adolescents grow up in homes that rely on extended family. This often results in uncles, aunts, cousins, and grandparents having power in the family and sharing responsibility in the care and rearing of children, as well as teaching skills and values (Baruth & Manning, 2009). Rivalry and competition are discouraged in families, and working for the benefit of the family is emphasized. Children are encouraged to help siblings, particularly the younger ones (Sinagatullin, 2003).

African Americans communicate in a style that can be characterized as frank. Their communication style consists of looks, gestures, and body language that are very direct. Changes in body language are evident in their communication style. Characteristically, individuals are not observed as directly facing each other in conversation or making eye contact. Typically, the speaker faces the individual while the listener looks off into the distance (Baruth & Manning, 2009; Shade, Kelly, & Oberg, 1997).

In my experience with African American children and adolescents, teachers earn their respect by relating to them as individuals. Although earning the respect of students is important with students from all cultural backgrounds, it is particularly important to earn the respect of African American students because they may openly confront an adult if respect is not earned (Sinagatullin, 2003). This type of challenging behavior may be stressful for beginning teachers who may not understand the role that culture plays in contributing to this type of behavior.

When teaching African American students, you should be aware of several implications. First, these students are typically kinesthetic learners who require movement in order to become engaged in learning. Second, you need to base your expectations on individual ability rather than stereotypical beliefs about African Americans and physical activity. Finally, you must take into consideration the impact of outside influences and life experiences that are a result of geographic location and socioeconomic status on student behavior (Culp, 2009).

Characteristics of Asian American Culture

The Asian American community includes immigrants from China, the Philippines, Japan, Vietnam, and other countries of Southeast Asia; however, they possess some common cultural values. Once again, it is important to understand that the following cultural characteristics may not be representative of all Asian Americans. The family is central in Asian culture, and Asian American families emphasize loyalty to the family. Parents stress their children's obligation to the family as well as their responsibility for abiding by family expectations. A strong emphasis is placed on the father as the head of the family, and additional value is placed on sons rather than daughters (Baruth & Manning, 2009). However, these characteristics may vary according to socioeconomic class and generational status.

Communication patterns of Asian Americans consist of both verbal and nonverbal communication. Many Asian Americans speak their native language in the home, while also speaking English. Asian American children and adolescents may have some difficulty with English as a result of the native language being the primary spoken language in homes.

Nonverbal communication and behaviors of Asian Americans are also important to understand. For example, the forward or backward leaning of the body indicates feelings. A backward lean indicates withdrawal from a conversation or topic, while a forward lean lets the speaker know that the listener is polite, concerned, and flexible (Baruth & Manning, 2009).

Within the Asian American culture, considerable emphasis is placed on education. Children are taught to be respectful of teachers and to consider them to be individuals of authority. Asian American parents teach children to value educational achievement, to respect authority, and to show self-control (Baruth & Manning, 2009). In school, Asian American children and adolescents perform better when they know

▶ Most likely, your class will include Anglo-American students, Hispanic students, African American students, Asian American students, and more. Members of each culture often share some general characteristics.

what is expected of them. They feel more comfortable in cooperative learning environments, and they benefit from positive reinforcement (Blair, 2003; Sinagatullin, 2003).

When teaching Asian American students, you should be aware of several implications. First, Asian Americans may not value physical education and may consider it as merely play (Sinagatullin, 2003). Second, you must consider the students' English proficiency; you should promote nonverbal communication in addition to encouraging students to improve their English language usage. Third, keep in mind that behavior that may seem to indicate indifference or disinterest (e.g., looking away or not volunteering an answer) is deemed appropriate for Asian learners and is in no way meant to be disrespectful. Finally, peer teaching can work well, especially when there are language difficulties (Culp, 2009).

Characteristics of Native American Culture

Although the media presents stereotypical images of Native Americans, this culture encompasses a very diverse group that varies significantly both physically and culturally. Some common characteristics can be identified when examining Native American culture, but you must use caution not to oversimplify and ignore individual differences.

A deep respect and commitment to family exists in the Native American culture, which places a high priority on both the immediate and extended family. The immediate and extended family, tribe, clan, and heritage all contribute to the children's cultural identity and play a role in their overall development (Baruth & Manning, 2009). The Native American family places importance on group welfare and trains children to be self-sufficient; however, self-sufficiency cannot come at the expense of family or tribal members. Native American adolescents seek social acceptance and approval from older and younger members of the family. They place family before self, and they respect their elders for their wisdom (Baruth & Manning, 2009).

Native American families teach cultural values to their children. They value being in harmony with nature and sharing, rather than saving, the basic necessities of life. They also value being identified as an important part of a group rather than for their individual accomplishments. Noncompetitive behavior is more acceptable than aggressive competition. Finally, patience is an important value among Native Americans and is considered more of a virtue than being quick to act (Baruth & Manning, 2009; Shade, Kelly, & Oberg, 1997).

The communication style of Native Americans is characterized by speaking softly and slowly. They typically avoid eye contact, and they seldom interject. They often offer nonverbal encouragement during communication, and they value nonverbal communication skills (Baruth & Manning, 2009; Shade, Kelly, & Oberg, 1997).

Educationally, Native American learners often feel more comfortable participating in class after they have had time to consider their responses or practice their skills, both inside and outside of class. Native American learners tend to be more comfortable in classrooms that are cooperative in nature and use small-group activities as instructional techniques (Fuller, 2001). In addition, the Native American cultural norm is to respect the teacher. This is demonstrated by Native American learners listening and typically not asking questions or responding (Culp, 2009).

When teaching Native American students, you should be aware of several implications. First, because Native Americans are more comfortable participating in class after they have time to think about their responses, you need to provide ample time for students to consider their answers. Second, you should not focus on competition because Native Americans place importance on maintaining harmony in a group and working cooperatively. Third, be aware that Native American learners tend not to make eye contact when they are withdrawing from the activity, are embarrassed, or are experiencing discomfort. Finally, Native American learners respond better to group praise rather than individual recognition because they take pride in the group receiving recognition (Culp, 2009).

Characteristics of Arab American Culture

Arab Americans have a culture that is rich with history and traditions. Arab Americans can trace their ancestry to people who emigrated from Arabic-speaking places in southwest Asia or northern Africa, a region known as the Middle East. Note that not all people in the Middle East are Arabs. For example, Iran is part of the Middle East; however, Iranians are considered Persians, not Arabs (Diliberto, 2009; Suleiman, 2000).

Before we begin the discussion of generalized cultural characteristics, it is important once again to caution the reader that not all Arab Americans fit within these cultural characteristics. The family is very important in the Arab American culture. Family members are taught to take great pride in their Arab heritage. A great sense of pride exists in individuals, families, communities, and society at large. In Arabic culture, people have a loyalty to their extended family, and group needs take precedence over individual needs and goals (Baruth & Manning, 2009; Nydell, 1996). The Arab family has been described as patriarchal and hierarchical with regard to age and sex. The male is viewed as the head of the family. As a result, children typically respect the father's authority and are encouraged to obey orders rather than explore ideas or thoughts with him. As a result of the patriarchal family structure, the differential treatment of boys is not uncommon, and girls are often expected to follow traditional female roles. However, variations in gender roles exist in Arab American families. Some of the variation in gender roles can be attributed to religion, the individual's country of origin, whether the family comes from a rural or urban area, and how long the individual's family has been in the United States (Baruth & Manning, 2009).

Arabs belong to many religions, including Islam, Christianity, Judaism, and others. You need to distinguish religion from culture. Arabs are connected by culture; however, they have different faiths. A common misconception is that Arab traditions are Islamic, or that Islam unifies all Arabs (Diliberto, 2009; Suleiman, 2000).

Although there is a great deal of diversity in the religions that Arab Americans practice, perhaps the least understood religion is Islam. In light of this, you need to gain some understanding of how Islam may affect teaching physical education. First, religious holidays such as Ramadan are very important to Muslims. During this religious holiday, Muslims do not eat, drink, or smoke between sunrise and sunset. You should be aware of students who are fasting during Ramadan because they may be weak and not as capable of performing in physical education. Second, Muslims must pray five times a day—at dawn, noon, afternoon, sunset, and night. Be sure to provide students with a place to pray if their prayer time coincides with their scheduled physical education class. Finally, some female Muslims may cover their head with a hijab (AlMunajjed, 1997; Nydell, 1996). Although this custom is observed by some Muslims, it is not universally observed by Muslim women, and it varies by region and class. For example, for women in Saudi Arabia, wearing a hijab is required for appearing in society (AlMunajjed, 1997). Muslim males may wear a keffiyeh, which is a traditional head covering (not tied to religion) worn to demonstrate their identity and pride in their culture (Culp, 2009). In physical education, an exception may need to be made in regard to dress and covering the head for Muslim students (Culp, 2009).

Because some Arab American families have been in the United States for generations, you should not assume that an Arab American knows Arabic any more than you would assume that other Americans can speak the language of their ethnic group; however, some Arab Americans may communicate in Arabic and may display characteristics typical of Arabic communication style.

Arabic communication style is characterized by repetition, indirectness, and elaborateness. Repetition is a major feature of Arabic discourse. Repeated words, phrases, and rhythms are used to move others to belief rather than the Western style of dialogue that uses ideas to persuade (Feghali, 1997).

Indirectness is another characteristic of Arabic communication style. Individuals may respond in agreeable or pleasant ways when direct or factual answers might prove embarrassing or distressing. Arabic speakers typically will not give a yes or no answer to a sensitive matter; the answer may often be somewhere in between (Feghali, 1997). Furthermore, Arabic speakers are very elaborate in their use of language. They typically use more words to communicate than speakers do in some other languages. When individuals communicate with each other, they often exaggerate so that they are not misunderstood (Feghali, 1997).

Students of Mixed Race

Several students in schools today may be of mixed race. In fact, the number of mixed-race students in schools is growing; in the next couple decades, students who enter postsecondary education will shift noticeably away from a monoracial norm to a more racially mixed cultural background (Renn, 2004). These students will bring experiences, interests, and needs that are different from those of monoracial students. You must have some understanding of the experiences and needs of students from these backgrounds in order to better serve them in the gymnasium.

These students may not all identify in the same way. Some may identify with one of their heritages, some with two or more, and some as *multiracial, biracial,* or another term that indicates being mixed (Renn, 2004). Depending on the manner in which students identify with their heritages, they may display the cultural characteristics of one or more groups. In addition, their identity may be influenced by other characteristics such as cultural knowledge, physical appearance, and gender (Renn, 2004).

To better understand the needs of your mixed-race students, you should get to know them and ask questions about how they identify with their different heritages. Getting to know their families may also be helpful. You can develop a relationship with the parents or guardians in an effort to help their child in physical education.

Culturally Responsive Teaching

Although learning about the various cultures of students is very important, you also need to take steps to become a culturally responsive teacher. A culturally responsive teacher possesses a frame of mind and uses teaching practices that are responsive to the culture, needs, interests, learning preferences, and abilities of each student (Lund & Tannehill, 2010).

You must learn about and embrace the cultural diversity of students. In addition, you should understand and be sensitive to the cultural identities of students, and you should promote students' appreciation of other cultures in society and the school environment. You can do several things to promote and develop an appreciation for cultural diversity.

First, you need to embrace the language of students. Language is part of culture. By working to include the different languages of your students, you will foster respect among students and create a more accepting climate in the gymnasium. The following list provides some suggestions for how to embrace the different languages of students.

▶ Learn to speak a few words or phrases in the languages of the students in your class.

▶ Do not show any bias toward the use of language other than English or against a student who speaks a different language, different dialect of English, or with a non-English accent.

▶ Create a literacy-rich environment in the gym by using posters with words in English, Spanish, sign language, or any other language.

▶ Give directions using English, Spanish, sign language, or other languages that your students speak.

▶ Speak slowly and clearly in whatever language you use in the gymnasium.

▶ Make demonstrations concrete and show the actions from different angles.

▶ Avoid jargon that might be misunderstood when speaking.

▶ Use an interpreter when communicating with parents unless they ask you to communicate in English.

▶ Use students who are bilingual as peer tutors or interpreters.

In addition to embracing the language of your students, you should develop an understanding of students' cultural communication styles. Cultural communication styles are made up of various nonverbal gestures and a group's preferences for interacting with others (Davis, 2007). If you do not know the nonverbal cues of your students, you might assume that students are being disrespectful or not listening. Furthermore, you may be unintentionally sending students the message that they are not important enough for the teacher to learn about their cultural communication styles. Here are some suggestions for learning about the communication styles of diverse learners:

▶ Observe your students' cultural groups in the gym and in public.

▶ Read books on body language and cultural communication.

▶ Attend conferences that include workshops about teaching physical education to students from different cultural groups.

▶ Do home visits and speak with students and their families.

▶ Talk with other teachers from diverse cultural groups.

▶ Ask your students questions.

Another way to enhance your relationship with your diverse learners is to teach a curriculum that has meaning and relevance to students. The curriculum should take into account the influence that students' culture may have on their perceptions of how meaningful they find physical education. Research results have indicated that physical education curriculum lacks meaning and relevance to some ethnic groups, and activity preferences vary among different ethnic groups (Cothran & Ennis, 2001; Hill & Cleven, 2005/2006; Tannehill & Zakrajsek, 1993).

To determine whether your curriculum is relevant to your students, you can survey students to find out what types of activities they may be interested in. Once you have collected and analyzed this data, you must take steps to implement these activities into your curriculum. Some of these activities may require you to do research so that you are able to teach an activity that you do not have much experience with. You may also have to remove some activities from the curriculum that you enjoy teaching; activities should be removed if they hold little or no meaning for your students.

Here are some other strategies that can help you become more culturally responsive and help you learn about the different cultures and languages of students:

▶ Talk with colleagues, parents, and friends who share the students' cultural background.

▶ Find out what social manners are important to the community, such as how children and adolescents interact with elders and peers.

▶ Read magazines and journals that focus on different communities, as well as community newspapers.

▶ Attend ethnic festivals and art shows and observe the social interactions and dress of the community members.

Although the aforementioned strategies are useful in helping you become culturally responsive, you need to realize that one of the most important things you can do is to develop rapport with students and their families. Developing relationships with students and their families will help you bridge the cultural divide that often exists between teachers and their diverse learners.

Disability

Students with disabilities are often marginalized in physical education (Blinde & McCallister, 1998; Hutzler, Fliess, Chacham, & van den Auweele, 2002). Often, physical education teachers fail to provide adequate accommodations for students. Research results indicate that the lack of accommodations for students with disabilities stems from inadequate training and from teachers lacking the experience and knowledge to successfully include students with disabilities (Hodge, Ammah, Casebolt, LaMaster, & O'Sullivan, 2004; Lieberman, Houston-Wilson, & Kozub, 2002). You should have the same expectations for all of your students, including students with and without special needs. Don't fall into the trap of having lower expectations for students with special needs than for your students who are able bodied.

More than likely, students with special needs will be included in your general physical education classes. At times, you may teach segregated classes consisting only of students with special needs. You may have students with a variety of special needs in your class, ranging from those who need minimal accommodations to help them succeed to students with severe disabilities. There are several strategies that you may use to teach students with special needs:

▶ Make sure that you understand students' disabilities and the accommodations they need in order to ensure their success in physical education.

▶ Students with and without disabilities can share the same physical education classes. Do make accommodations for those with special needs, but take care to include everyone and have the same expectations of students.

▶ Meet with parents and the special education teacher to discuss any concerns about the student.

▶ Participate in the IEP process and write the physical education section of the IEPs for your students.

▶ Research and adapt content as well as equipment for students.

▶ Develop a positive working relationship with the special education teacher, paraeducator, occupational therapist, and physical therapist to ensure consistency and success in the gymnasium.

Figures 7.1 and 7.2 provide several adapted physical education books and websites that may be helpful in providing appropriate instruction to students with special needs. In addition to examining these resources, you can seek consultation with an adapted physical education specialist or a college or university faculty member who specializes in adapted physical education.

Sherrill, C. (2004). *Adapted physical activity, recreation, and sport: Crossdisciplinary and lifespan* (6th ed.). New York: McGraw-Hill.

Winnick, J.P. (Ed). (2011). *Adapted physical education and sport* (5th ed.). Champaign, IL: Human Kinetics.

National Consortium for Physical Education and Recreation for Individuals With Disabilities, Kelly, L. (Ed). (2006). *Adapted physical education national standards* (2nd ed.). Champaign, IL: Human Kinetics.

Horvat, M., Block, M., & Kelly, L. (2007). *Developmental and adapted physical activity assessment.* Champaign, IL: Human Kinetics.

Kasser, S.L., & Lytle, R.K. (2005). *Inclusive physical activity: A lifetime of opportunities.* Champaign, IL: Human Kinetics.

McCall, R.M., & Craft, D.H. (2000). *Moving with a purpose: Developing programs for preschoolers of all abilities.* Champaign, IL: Human Kinetics.

Lieberman, L.J. (Ed). (2007). *Paraeducators in physical education: A training guide to roles and responsibilities.* Champaign, IL: Human Kinetics.

Lieberman, L.J., & Houston-Wilson, C. (2002). *Strategies for inclusion: A handbook for physical educators.* Champaign, IL: Human Kinetics.

▶ **FIGURE 7.1** Adapted physical education books.

Adapted Physical Education National Standards (www.apens.
org)

American Association for Physical Activity and Recreation (www.
aahperd.org/aapar)

American Association of Adapted Sports Programs (www.aaasp.
org)

National Center on Physical Activity and Disability (www.ncpad.
org)

PALAESTRA Journal (www.palaestra.com)

Project Inspire (www.twu.edu/INSPIRE)

Special Olympics (www.specialolympics.org)

Wheelchair and Ambulatory Sports, USA (www.wsusa.org)

▶ **FIGURE 7.2** Adapted physical education websites.

Meeting Individual Differences

All students are individuals who have different needs; however, some students' needs require modification of activities in order for the students to be successful in physical education. Activity modifications can be broken down into four categories: equipment, rules, environment, and instruction (Lieberman & Houston-Wilson, 2002). For example, if a student has a visual impairment, equipment could be brightly colored or could emit a sound. If a student is lacking in muscular strength, the equipment could be lighter in weight.

When modifying an activity, you should try to keep it as close to the traditional activity as possible. Modifications should be limited to those necessary to meet individual needs; you must keep in mind the educational experiences of both the students needing the modification and their classmates (Collier, 2005).

Working With Paraeducators

Paraeducators are professionals who assist the special education teacher as well as the physical education teacher. Although paraeducators can be a great asset to you, they need to be trained. This training may be provided through a school district or by individual physical education teachers.

Expectations and responsibilities vary for paraeducators in physical education; however, you can consider several responsibilities and expectations for the paraeducators in your class. For example, paraeducators should have a working knowledge of student movement. They should also be knowledgeable about important considerations regarding a student's disability while in an indoor or outdoor movement environment. In addition, the paraprofessional needs to know the student's strengths and weaknesses, as well as the student's present level of performance, goals, and objectives (Lieberman, 2007).

Paraeducators should also know the units of instruction and lesson plans for the physical education class. You may want to plan lessons with the paraeducator or at least speak with the paraeducator in advance about the content of the lesson and what the paraeducator needs to do during the lesson. The paraeducator also needs to keep you up to date on any pertinent information regarding students with disabilities that may affect student performance in physical education. Finally, paraeducators are expected to dress for activity and to actively participate with students. They need to be actively involved in the class in order to assist students with disabilities as well as able-bodied students if need be (Lieberman, 2007). The following tips may help you when working with paraeducators (Lieberman, 2007):

▶ Meet with paraeducators on a regular basis to plan instruction.

▶ Decide with the paraeducators what their role should be in each lesson, but remain flexible to accommodate changes during the lesson.

▶ Clarify what the paraeducators need to do in regard to discipline for students who are misbehaving.

▶ Communicate and collaborate with the paraeducators to implement the IEP goals for students.

▶ Demonstrate respect for paraeducators and communicate that you value their input as well as their contributions to individual students and the entire class.

▶ Discuss with the paraeducators how you would like them to address safety issues in physical education.

Gender

The manner in which teachers treat males and females in physical education also affects student learning. Many teachers say that they are gender blind; however, this may be impossible because one of the first things you see as a teacher is that some students are males and some are females. Still, many teachers believe that they teach students the same way regardless of gender. But do they? Research results have indicated that teachers do not treat males and females in the same manner during physical education class. For example, research results have indicated that teachers display gender-biased perceptions and explanations for student behavior (Griffin, 1985; Macdonald, 1990) and that physical education teachers interact with boys more than girls during physical education (Dunbar & O'Sullivan, 1986).

The terms *gender* and *sex* are often used interchangeably; however, the meanings and use of these terms differ. Sex refers to the biological differences between males and females; whereas gender refers to the social, cultural, and psychological aspects that pertain to the traits, norms, roles, and stereotypes considered typical for those whom society has designated as male or female (Doyle & Paludi, 1998).

Gender identity is learned, and it is often reinforced through the curriculum and actions of the physical education teacher. Frequently, females are stereotyped as not being as good in sports and physical activity as males. Physical education teachers often reinforce this message by saying things such as "You throw like a girl" or "Stop being such a girl!" Males are not immune from gender bias. Sometimes males are singled out for misbehaving more than females. For example, African American females often have an advantage in classrooms because teachers perceive them to be better behaved than African American males. As a result, African American males are treated as troublemakers (Delpit, 1995).

Physical education teachers are often unaware of their gender bias in the gymnasium. For example, how many times do physical educators use the term *guys*? As a beginning teacher, I had an experience that changed the way I addressed students. One day in a sixth grade class, I said, "When I say go, I would like you guys to walk over and get a basketball, move into general space, and put the ball on the floor between your ankles. Go!" All of the students except for one girl followed my directions. I asked the girl to get up and get a basketball, but she responded, "I didn't think you were talking to me because I am not a guy." I learned my lesson and started addressing students as "folks." I was subconsciously being biased against female students in my gymnasium by referring to them as "guys." To promote a more gender equitable environment in my gymnasium, I had to change the way I addressed students.

Using the term *guys* is one example of how language can promote gender inequities. Unfortunately, your use of language can send implicit messages that females are less competent than males. For example, terminology such as *good sportsmanship* can be replaced by *good sporting behavior* or *fair play*. Instead of using terminology such as *girl push-ups,* use the term *modified push-ups*. You should also develop a culture that allows both males and females to perform modified push-ups. The following tips can help you create a more gender equitable classroom.

▶ Some teachers inadvertently give verbal or nonverbal cues that reinforce gender stereotypes, such as the belief that boys are better at basketball than girls are.

▶ Communicate the same expectations to both males and females.

▶ Use both genders in demonstrations.

▶ Use language that includes both genders. Replace "guys" with "folks" or "ladies and gentlemen."

▶ Give feedback to both males and females.

▶ Ensure that groups are gender balanced.

▶ Ensure that jobs such as picking up equipment or moving equipment such as mats are assigned to both genders.

▶ Do not ignore remarks that ridicule one gender or the other, such as "You throw like a girl."

▶ Use gender-neutral terms such as *good sporting behavior* instead of *good sportsmanship.*

▶ Discuss the contributions and the role of women in sport.

▶ Do not divide students into groups or teams based on gender.

▶ Make a conscious effort to comment equally on all students' responses and contributions in the gymnasium.

Sexual Orientation

The attitudes toward lesbian, gay, bisexual, and transgender (LGBT) students in schools can be less than accepting. Since 1999, the Gay, Lesbian, and Straight Education Network (GLSEN), a national organization focused on ensuring safe schools for all students regardless of sexual orientation or gender identity or expression, has surveyed LGBT students in secondary schools regarding their perceptions of school climate. Results from a 2007 report from GLSEN (Kosciw, Diaz, & Greytak, 2008) indicated the following:

▶ 73.6 percent of students heard homophobic remarks frequently or often.

▶ 86.2 percent reported being verbally harassed (e.g., called names or threatened) as a result of their sexual orientation.

▶ 22.1 percent reported being physically assaulted (e.g., punched, kicked, or injured with a weapon) because of their sexual orientation.

▶ 44.1 percent reported being physically harassed (being pushed or shoved) because of their sexual orientation.

▶ Almost 61 percent of the students who were harassed or assaulted in school did not report the incident to school staff, believing that little or no action would be taken or the situation would become worse if reported.

▶ A little over 31 percent of students who reported incidents indicated that the school staff did nothing in response.

These statistics are evidence of the harassment and violence that LGBT students face daily in school as a result of homophobia. Homophobia affects all people—people of different sexual orientations, genders, and ages. Homophobia in schools and a lack of teacher intervention are particularly troublesome because research has indicated that LGBT youth may be at a higher risk for depression, suicide, and negative risk-taking behaviors (Bontempo & D'Augelli, 2002; DuRant, Krowchuk, & Senal, 1998).

Sadly, physical education is often an environment that exacerbates homophobia. Males often view physical education and sport as a place to demonstrate their masculinity and athletic prowess. In addition, some females shy away from physical education and physical activity because they fear that showing a level of competence in physical activities will cause their sexual orientation to be in question.

One common act of homophobia that occurs in the gymnasium is verbal name calling using words such as *faggot* and *dyke*. Homophobic name calling is pervasive. I remember the first time I had a student call another student a faggot. The student was a third grader, and he was upset because the other student did not want to be his partner. I recognized the opportunity as a teachable moment and had a discussion with the student about what he had said and how it was inappropriate. Basically, I spoke to him about other types of name calling that had occurred in class, such as students calling people names because of the size of their body or because of the color of their skin. We talked about how this was hurtful to people and how we need to be accepting of individual differences in people. I asked him why he called the student a faggot. He replied that he did not know, but that his big brother called people he was mad at a faggot, so he thought he would do the same.

As a teacher, you must intervene when a student makes a homophobic statement. By not intervening, you make a decision that hurts students. By choosing to intervene when you hear a homophobic slur, you will help students. Be sure to use these interventions as teachable moments and tell students how the remark made you feel. In addition, use this opportunity as a jumping-off point for meaningful conversations about how remarks such as these affect students and the class as a whole in physical education.

Many teachers are not comfortable confronting students who use homophobic name calling to humiliate other students. Teachers do not realize that this sort of name calling should be dealt with in the same way as other name calling. In my gymnasium, I instituted a "no hate language" policy. This policy specified that students were not to call other students names that had to do with the color of their skin, their religion, body size, disability, sexual orientation, dress, family status, and so on. I developed and instituted this policy because I believed that it was my obligation as a teacher to teach children about all forms of discrimination.

You can take several steps to counteract homophobia in the gymnasium. For example, you need to educate yourself about homophobia. You can do this by attending workshops on homophobia, reading books and other educational material, and exploring websites such as www.glsen.org (the site for the Gay, Lesbian, and Straight Education Network). Other helpful activities include viewing films and attending events that are focused on LGBT issues, as well as talking with friends, family, and colleagues about homophobia.

Another way to counteract homophobia in the gymnasium is to be an ally for gay and lesbian colleagues and students. Let them know that you are supportive of them as individuals. If you are LGBT, be as out as you can be; however, this may not be feasible in all situations and may jeopardize an untenured teacher's job security. Nonetheless, a visible LGBT person who presents him- or herself in a positive light will help contradict stereotypes and myths regarding LGBT people. Here are some more ideas for counteracting homophobia in the gymnasium:

▶ Establish guidelines for name calling, harassment, and teasing and treat homophobic name calling as you would racial, gender, religious, and other types of discriminatory name calling. Enforce these guidelines gently but firmly in an educational manner.

▶ Express your dissatisfaction when students tell homophobic jokes. Tell the students that it is not appropriate to make jokes about any group.

▶ Express your dissatisfaction when students say, "That's so gay." Tell the students that although that statement is slang, it is offensive to LGBT individuals.

▶ When students engage in homophobic name calling, discuss and explore the issue with students. This can be done by asking questions such as "What does that word mean to you?" "What did your classmate do to make you call her that?" or "How do you feel if someone calls you that name?"

▶ Model non-heterosexist behaviors. For example, don't joke or tease someone for nontraditional gender behaviors.

▶ Support and promote school policies that directly address the prevention of LGBT bullying and harassment in order to create better learning environments for LGBT students.

▶ Support Gay-Straight Alliance clubs.

▶ Join a local GLSEN chapter.

Summary

Diversity in physical education is a very complex issue. Diversity contains several components that intersect with each other in a manner that contributes to different experiences for each individual student. Aspects of diversity that were discussed in the chapter include culture, language, disability, gender, and sexual orientation. Each of these components of diversity influences what happens in a gymnasium and influences interactions among students as well as between the teacher and students.

You need to have a basic understanding of diversity and how certain aspects of diversity affect the teaching-learning environment. Remember, the content of this chapter is intended to provide a basic understanding of diversity. As you move through your career, you should continue to build your knowledge base regarding diversity and should reflect on how the diversity of your students and your own diversity affect the learning process.

DISCUSSION QUESTIONS

1. What is culture? How do students' cultural backgrounds affect the teaching-learning environment in the gymnasium?

2. Why is it important to understand how your personal diversity and experiences affect the teaching-learning environment in the gymnasium?

3. Why is it important to have a basic understanding of the cultural characteristics of various ethnic groups?

4. Why do you need to have an understanding of differences related to gender, disability, and sexual orientation in order to be an effective teacher?

Assessment: Who Am I?

1. Who am I?

2. What is my racial and ethnic background?

3. What is my cultural background?

4. What traditions or holidays do I celebrate that are related to my culture?

5. What is my educational background?

6. What is my socioeconomic level?

7. What is my religion?

8. What is my sexual orientation?

9. How have my family and community shaped who I am as a person?

10. How does my background influence my interactions with students?

From A. James, 2013, *Survive and thrive as a physical educator: Strategies for the first year and beyond* (Champaign, IL: Human Kinetics).

Assessment: Who Are My Students?

1. Who are my students?

2. What is important to the community in which my students live?

3. What is the cultural background of my students?

4. What is the socioeconomic level of my students' families?

5. What is the educational background of my students' parents?

6. What religions do my students and their parents practice?

7. How have my students' family and community background shaped them into the people they are?

8. How do my students' backgrounds influence how they interact with me?

From A. James, 2013, *Survive and thrive as a physical educator: Strategies for the first year and beyond* (Champaign, IL: Human Kinetics).

CHAPTER 8

Navigating the School as a Workplace

A beginning physical education teacher will struggle with various issues related to being a teacher in a school. The school itself as a workplace has its own unique challenges, such as dealing with workplace conditions, developing relationships with colleagues, and gaining insight into the bureaucracy that operates in all schools.

A school functions as a small community within the larger school district. A school has its own rules, social groups, and customs. You must gain a level of knowledge regarding how the school community works and what you need to do to become a thriving member of that community. To become a successful member of this community you must continue to develop as a teacher, and in order to do so, you must understand the socializing role of the school.

The School as a Socializing Agent

A school is an organization that attempts to socialize its new members. Some of this socialization is necessary as well as beneficial. For example, it is good for you to be socialized into some school traditions, such as being an active participant at faculty meetings and interacting with parents and guardians at open house events. The school will shape you as a beginning teacher, so you should consider how you will respond to the socializing forces.

Essentially, new physical education teachers will react to socializing factors in the school workplace in one of three ways. Lawson (1989) identified these orientations that were first described by Van Maanen and Schein (1979) as custodial orientation, content innovative, and role innovative.

The custodial orientation causes beginning teachers to believe that it is in their best interest to abide by and preserve existing policies and practices in physical education (Lawson, 1989). They may take the viewpoint that it is better to go along to get along. The custodial orientation functions to maintain the status quo. You may find that your belief system is at odds with this orientation, and you may have some reservations about adopting the custodial orientation. However, you may believe that fitting in and not rocking the boat are more important and that you can always go back and do things differently once you are tenured. If you respond in this way, you may find that your initial feelings of enthusiasm and excitement about teaching physical education are turning to feelings of anxiety and unhappiness with your career choice.

In talking with directors of physical education, I have found that they do not want beginning teachers to follow this path. Many have expressed to me that they hire young teachers with the expectation that those teachers will come in and help make changes that will enhance the physical education program. The directors also indicated that they want new teachers to help their more seasoned colleagues move toward teaching physical education in a manner that is cutting edge and current.

The second way you can react to socializing factors is to be content innovative, which involves changing selected ways that teaching is performed in physical education (Lawson, 1989). For example, a teacher who is content innovative may use teaching advances such as curriculum models or may develop an assessment system that emphasizes student learning. Teachers who are content innovative are able to create some change by resisting being socialized to accept the existing system (i.e., they resist the custodial orientation).

The third way you can respond to socialization in the workplace is by being role innovative, which means that you transform physical education and the manner in which physical education and the physical education teacher are viewed in the school (Lawson, 1989). For example, you can be role innovative by planning and teaching a sequential curriculum that is focused on learning instead of just playing games that have little purpose. In addition, you could use assessments that enhance the teaching-learning process. Teachers who share assessments with students throughout instruction are able to communicate their expectations for learning to the students; these teachers are also able to communicate to students and their parents that the grades in physical education are based on student learning rather than dressing and participation. Finally, you can take a visible role on committees in the school, such as the wellness committee. Or, you can start physical activity programs for students, faculty, staff, and community members outside of the school day to promote physical education. Resource 8.1 provides a graphic organizer that enables you to list the actions you will take to adopt a content-innovative or role-innovative orientation to school socialization.

At some schools, new teachers will encounter socializing tactics that make it very difficult for them to be content or role innovative. Factors such as pressure from colleagues to do less work, colleagues and administrators who do not value physical education, and students themselves may make it difficult for you to teach in the manner that you were taught in your preservice education. For example, I did a lot of assessment, which made several of my colleagues uncomfortable. They expressed that it made them look bad to administrators because they did not do assessment. In addition, these colleagues often expressed negative comments about curriculum innovations and lesson ideas that I was implementing because these innovations were different and required extra work.

Students also had a role in socializing me as a beginning teacher. My first year as a teacher, I replaced a teacher who retired; however, for the previous year, this teacher worked only one day a week to use up sick leave that the district would not buy out. On the other days of the week, the students had substitute teachers. Needless to say, when I began teaching, the students were resistant to any structure or instruction that focused on student learning. Most of the resistance came from the older students. After that year, the older students moved to the middle school, and the following year was much better.

Although I struggled to respond to socializing factors such as students and resistant colleagues, I was successful by being role innovative. My success was the result of many things; however, I attribute most of my success to three factors:

1. I believed that my undergraduate education prepared me to teach effectively.
2. I had a supportive administrator.
3. I became very involved in all aspects of the school, including serving on committees, coordinating physical activity programs outside of the school day, and taking every opportunity to advocate for physical education with colleagues, administrators, and parents.

Certain strategies can be used to deal with socialization tactics in a way that enables you to take on an innovative orientation. Obviously, you have to consider things such as building relationships with colleagues and administrators as well as being able to carry out the duties associated with being a teacher. Although it is difficult to resist the socializing forces of the school, you can make choices that allow you to respond to socialization without taking the custodial orientation. First and foremost, you must be proactive and seek the help you need to be successful and to deal with issues you encounter.

Next, talk with your administrators about your ideas and try to gain their support for doing different things with the physical education program. Supportive administrators are instrumental in helping you foster an innovative orientation toward socialization. Keep in mind that although colleagues can exert a strong socializing force on you, they do not play a role in tenure decisions. All too often, beginning teachers believe that they will not get tenure if they do not fit in and do what their colleagues do, even if their colleagues do not use best practices. The reality is that the administrators who you work with make tenure decisions, not your colleagues.

In addition, you should join professional organizations, gather information from their websites, and attend professional conferences to cultivate an innovative orientation toward socialization. Stay abreast of current developments in physical education so that you can share them with colleagues and administrators.

Furthermore, you must be an advocate for physical education in and out of school. In school, you should offer opportunities for physical education and physical activity before and after school. For example, I offered before-school physical education for students who arrived at school early and had nowhere else to go. I also organized and supervised after-school programs that included intramural activities as well as noncompetitive physical activity opportunities. Outside of school, you can advocate by doing presentations for the school board and community groups about the importance of physical education. Furthermore, you can educate yourself about legislation that affects physical education and lobby members of the senate and congress to support positive legislation.

Teacher Development

In addition to understanding the socialization that occurs in a school, you need to develop an understanding of the stages of teacher development. You have already entered into the stages of professional development by developing professional skills and dispositions during your preservice education. For example, preservice training includes instruction regarding how to write lesson plans and unit plans, how to manage a classroom, how to use various instructional strategies, and how to teach in a way that maximizes physical activity. According to Katz (1972), teacher development includes four stages: the survival stage, consolidation stage, renewal stage, and maturity stage.

Survival Stage

The first phase of teacher development that you encounter after your preservice education is called the survival stage, which is often referred to as the *induction stage* (Katz, 1972; Letven, 1992). This is the stage that most beginning teachers are engaged in during their first year of teaching. During this stage, beginning teachers are socialized into the system. It is a period when a new teacher strives for acceptance by students, peers, and supervisors and attempts to achieve a comfort and security level in dealing with everyday issues (Letven, 1992). During this stage, you will need a great deal of assistance and encouragement to help you adapt to being a physical education teacher.

In the survival stage, you will likely encounter what has been termed reality shock. Reality shock is what happens when beginning teachers realize that what they learned in their preservice teacher education does not always work in their teaching setting (Lawson, 1989). As a result, you may feel overwhelmed and inadequate.

I experienced reality shock firsthand when I began my first teaching job in Cincinnati. I believed that I was well prepared from my preservice education; however, I was not equipped to teach students from diverse backgrounds, and I did not have strategies for addressing many of the issues presented in the classroom as a result of differences in race, culture, and socioeconomic status. Although I tried to teach lessons that focused on student learning and included skill development, this was a struggle because of issues related to nonparticipation and inappropriate behavior, which often interrupted instruction and made teaching stressful.

Be aware that reality shock is a certainty for most novice teachers. You must be prepared for the contradictions between teacher education and the school practices at your school. For example, as a preservice teacher, you were taught the importance of assessing students; however, your colleagues may not value assessment and may choose to do little if any assessment. What should you do? Beginning teachers are often torn between wanting to fit in with new colleagues and doing what they believe is the best practice. At this point, you will have to make a

▶ New physical education teachers can face reality shock when they realize that a seemingly simple task, such as organizing students, can be more complicated than they expected.

decision. Do you teach the way you were taught, or do you take your cues from the other teachers to conform and fit in?

This is an important decision, because if you choose to conform to school practices that are not considered best practices, the so-called washout effect begins. This happens when the effects of teacher education are diminished. It has been described as a process where school practices and comments from colleagues gradually break down the effects of teacher education (Blankenship & Coleman, 2009; Lawson, 1989; Zeichner & Tabachnik, 1981). As a result of this process, physical education as a subject will not change, and physical educators have little chance to enhance their impact on student learning.

Consolidation Stage

By the second year of teaching, most teachers have entered the consolidation stage and have begun to focus on the needs of individual children (Katz, 1972). Burke and McDonnell (1992) refer to this stage as the competency-building stage. Teachers work hard and strive to improve their teaching skill by seeking different materials and teaching strategies. They see their job as challenging; however, they are eager to improve their repertoire of skills (Burke & McDonnell, 1992).

In this stage, you will be eager to improve; you should ask questions of a trusted colleague and explore new ideas. At this point, you will still be struggling with several issues. For example, you may struggle with how you are perceived as a teacher in the school. Students and other teachers often marginalize physical education teachers and relegate them to second-class citizenship in the school community.

Renewal Stage

The next stage of teacher development is the renewal stage (Katz, 1972). Teachers at this stage begin to look for new ideas that provide variety in the teaching setting. They typically become more interested in new teaching ideas and practices. They assign a great deal of value to attending conferences and workshops in search of new teaching ideas and practices. In addition, they also find value in reading journals and exchanging ideas with other colleagues who are interested in enhancing the teaching-learning environment in their gymnasium (Stroot & Whipple, 2003).

Maturity Stage

The final stage of teacher development is the maturity stage (Katz, 1972). In this stage, teachers begin to focus on their insights, perspectives, and beliefs about teaching children and adolescents. Teachers at this stage of development should share their ideas and concerns with other teachers who are also at this stage of development. By doing so, they will continue to grow and improve as teachers and will be better equipped to avoid experiencing burnout (Stroot & Whipple, 2003).

Burnout

Teachers experience burnout as a result of having stress, becoming disillusioned with teaching as a profession, and constantly battling the lack of status that physical education typically has in schools. Burnout is a state of mental and physical exhaustion as a result of long-term stress (Joseph, 2000). A teacher approaching burnout may experience any of the following:

▶ Lacking enthusiasm to teach physical education

▶ Being critical of your colleagues

▶ Being critical of your students

▶ Avoiding people associated with your job

▶ Arriving late or missing meetings at work

▶ Taking frequent "mental health" days

▶ Feeling sick more often

▶ Waking up and wishing you did not have to go to work

▶ Being irritable and having little patience with your colleagues or students

▶ Considering changing your career path

The causes of burnout are complex and intertwined, and it is difficult to identify one specific factor that contributes to burnout. Burnout is related to how a person deals with the stressors of teaching. Part of this stress is a result of teachers having roles (in addition to the role of teacher) that may be in conflict with each other.

As a teacher, the roles you have may include being a counselor and a disciplinarian. In addition, you may be a coach, spouse, partner, parent, son, daughter, aunt, uncle, and so on. As a result of having so many roles at one time, you may experience role overload. Role overload may occur when you do not have the time, energy, or ability to adequately fulfill all of the expectations associated with each of your roles. Furthermore, role conflict occurs when one role directly contradicts the expectations of another (Bain & Wendt, 1983).

For example, one role that many physical education teachers have is the role of coach. Teachers who are coaching often put in long days and work on weekends. The time demands can place a great deal of stress on teachers, which may lead them to minimize their role and responsibilities as a teacher and focus on coaching. This experience has been referred to as the teacher–coach conflict. Typically, this conflict occurs because the coaching role often reaps more rewards and greater status than teaching physical education. For example, I can remember several times when people complimented me and my team on a job well done; however, I never had someone walk up to me and tell me what a great throwing and catching lesson I taught. The irony of this for me was that my influence as a coach was only on a few players, whereas I influenced hundreds of students on a daily basis as a teacher. It always made me a little sad that people put more value on a successful athletic team than on student learning in physical education.

The teacher–coach conflict is real, and all physical educators who coach will experience it to some degree. You must recognize that the stress of the workload created by teaching and coaching at the same time can harm your job performance as a teacher and coach and possibly dampen your enthusiasm for teaching.

Another factor that contributes to burnout is that your teacher education training may not have prepared you to deal with the realities of teaching. Preservice teacher training programs do a very nice job of helping teachers develop skills such as planning and assessing; however, you may not have been prepared for the depth and breadth of teaching responsibilities as well as for the lack of status that physical educators have in the school. In the end, this may result in you having unrealistic expectations and finding that your training has not addressed the reality of teaching.

Student misbehavior is another factor that contributes to the stress and burnout of teachers. The stress of disruptive student behavior has changed a great deal over the past several decades. Today it is not uncommon for students to threaten and physically or verbally assault teachers. One way to alleviate the stress caused by student misbehavior is to create and implement a good classroom management plan that contains specific techniques for addressing disciplinary issues. A classroom management plan helps set boundaries for students in terms of what is acceptable behavior and what is not. When students behave in an acceptable manner, this greatly reduces the negative stress that the teacher experiences. Chapter 5 provided information about creating an effective classroom management plan.

Parents can also be a source of stress for teachers. Many parents are quite supportive of teachers in the school; however, parents can also be confrontational, which leads to added stress for the teacher. At times parents can be critical of a teacher and may even be verbally abusive. They may suggest that physical education is not a "real" subject or that you do not teach well enough or do not deal with situations correctly.

▶ The teacher–coach conflict can cause a physical education teacher to feel burned out if her coaching responsibilities demand a great deal of her time and effort.

This type of criticism will be upsetting to you, which may result in increased levels of stress that may affect your ability and desire to teach.

You need to develop skills and strategies to cope with stress in the workplace before you come to a personal breaking point and experience burnout. People cope with stress in many ways. Some of these methods are constructive and positive, while others are negative. Your success in dealing with stressors lies in your choice of coping mechanisms. You need to adopt positive coping mechanisms and recognize negative coping mechanisms that are counterproductive. For example, positive coping mechanisms include understanding the issues that you are facing and seeking help in addressing these issues. Another positive coping mechanism is not taking everything personally that people may say or do. Negative coping mechanisms may ease the crisis, but they can hurt you in the long run. Examples of negative coping mechanisms include engaging in risky behavior (such as drinking alcohol excessively), withdrawing from the situation, or blaming others such as students or administrators for issues associated with the job.

Dealing With the Stress of the Teacher–Coach Conflict

Although the stress created by the teacher–coach conflict cannot be avoided, there are strategies that can minimize its effects. One strategy is to set limits on how you will fulfill the expectations of both roles. For example, although I held both positions and had to put time and energy into both roles, I decided that my primary role during the school day was to be a teacher. Being a coach was my secondary role. I focused on teaching and planning for teaching during the school day, which meant that practice planning and watching game films did not happen during the school day. I budgeted time to plan for practices and watch game film on weekends and in the evening. This system allowed me to make teaching my focus during the school day and to focus on coaching during and after athletic practices.

Teachers need to be very careful if they choose to focus on coaching more than teaching. Although there are rewards and status associated with being a coach, those rewards and status are diminished greatly when a coach is not winning. Second, few people coach for their entire teaching career because the time commitment to coach, the emotional demands, and the pressure to win often become too much of a strain.

Techniques for Avoiding Burnout

One way to deal with stress and avoid burnout is to engage in professional development and set professional goals. Both will be discussed in detail in chapter 10. Teachers who have professional goals and participate in professional development activities are less prone to suffer from burnout.

A lot of the negative stress that beginning teachers suffer from is a result of a lack of time. Improving time management skills could significantly reduce the stress. One way to do this is to make a schedule and follow a timetable. You may want to create daily, weekly, and monthly timetables. Determine the number of hours you will need to prepare for teaching and coaching as well as how much time you need for yourself and your family. Then create a timetable that allocates enough time to get these things done.

You should also make daily lists of tasks that need to be completed and attach specific times that these tasks will be accomplished. Creating lists such as these will remind you what you need to do and will eliminate the stress caused by thinking you forgot something.

In addition to stress-relieving techniques that are related to teaching physical education, other techniques that involve your personal life and health are also important for alleviating stress. One technique is to develop a support group that consists of physical education colleagues as well as colleagues who teach in other areas. This support group allows you to network with other professionals and gain social support. Sharing experiences with others can lead to new insights about coping with various stressors. For example, if you are experiencing difficulty with a student who is misbehaving, one of your colleagues may have had a similar experience and may be able to give advice that would improve the situation.

Although having a support group that consists of professional colleagues is important, you also need to have strong support from family and friends. Family and friends may not completely understand the stresses involved with being a teacher, but their support can help make you more resilient and less susceptible to stress.

In addition, you must take care of yourself. Be sure to eat a well-balanced diet and develop eating habits that reduce the negative effects of stress. Exercise is important in fighting stress. Exercise assists in dealing with stress because it helps you to maintain a level of health and fitness that allows you not only to do your job but also to have a higher quality of life. Moreover, exercise takes your mind off of things that cause negative stress. It can also be a social activity. For example, joining a gym or participating on recreational sport teams allows you to be physically active and develop friendships with people who could become part of a support group.

Sleep is another weapon you can use to fight stress. Getting enough sleep is very important. Some people require more sleep than others; however, although the number of hours of sleep a person gets may vary, the quality of that sleep is very important.

Finally, relaxation techniques are important habits that you can use to reduce stress. Mastering a relaxation technique such as meditation is a great investment in health, and most people believe they are better able to cope with stress after a period of relaxation. Resource 8.2 is an organizer that will help you develop a plan to avoid burnout.

Summary

As a beginning teacher, you need to have an understanding of the school as a workplace. You may not have given serious thought to the school being a workplace; a school as a place of work is very different from your perceptions of a school when you were a student.

Schools and the people in the school community socialize beginning teachers into the school as a workplace. You must recognize this process of socialization and must be an active participant who considers how the socializing influences are affecting your performance as a physical education teacher.

In addition, you need to understand the stages of development that you will go through as a beginning teacher and throughout your career. Unfortunately, you may experience reality shock and washout to some degree; however, by being aware of these issues, you can take steps to deal with them.

In addition to understanding teacher development, you must have an understanding of what burnout is and what you can do to avoid it. Burnout is a very real condition that many teachers experience at some point in their careers. Several factors interact to cause a teacher to experience burnout. These factors include role conflict and overload, student misbehavior, negative interactions with parents, and how a teacher deals with stress.

You should take steps to develop strategies for avoiding burnout throughout your teaching career. Effective strategies include having a plan for how you will deal with the teacher–coach conflict, pursuing professional development activities, engaging in effective time management, and having social support from colleagues, family, and friends. In addition, you should engage in healthy habits such as eating a healthy diet, getting enough sleep, and engaging in daily exercise.

DISCUSSION QUESTIONS

1. What are the three ways that a beginning teacher can respond to the socializing influence of the school? What steps will you take to deal with the socializing effects of the school?

2. What is reality shock? How will you prepare yourself to deal with reality shock?

3. What is the washout effect? What steps will you take to avoid the washout effect?

4. What is the teacher–coach conflict? What is your plan for dealing with the teacher–coach conflict?

5. What is burnout? What steps will you take as a teacher to avoid burnout?

Actions to Help You Adopt a Content-Innovative or Role-Innovative Orientation to School Socialization

Actions to adopt content-innovative orientation to school socialization

Actions to adopt role-innovative orientation to school socialization

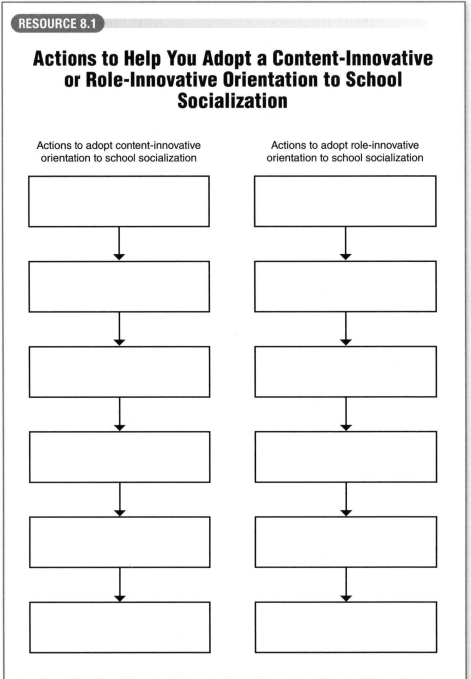

From A. James, 2013, *Survive and thrive as a physical educator: Strategies for the first year and beyond* (Champaign, IL: Human Kinetics).

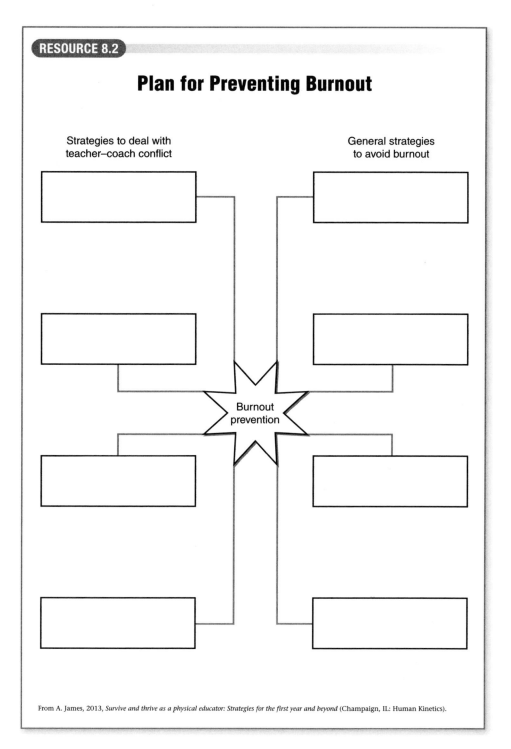

Plan for Preventing Burnout

Strategies to deal with
teacher–coach conflict

General strategies
to avoid burnout

Burnout
prevention

From A. James, 2013, *Survive and thrive as a physical educator: Strategies for the first year and beyond* (Champaign, IL: Human Kinetics).

CHAPTER 9

Developing Relationships With Parents

A beginning teacher has little or no experience in dealing with students' parents; however, this is a crucial aspect of your job. Parents' involvement in their child's school life is critical to the success of students, and it is also a big factor in your ability to be an effective teacher.

When you are able to develop relationships with parents and actively recruit them to be involved and aware of what happens at their child's school, you are more apt to have students who perform well and are well behaved. Developing relationships with parents or guardians of your students is not always easy. It often takes a great deal of time and effort.

Keep in mind that children in today's society may have families that differ in structure from yours. Children today may live in one-parent households or in households with stepparents. Some children may have adoptive parents or live in foster care settings. Other children may have same-sex parents, while others may live with relatives or guardians.

Several issues may impede or slow the development of a teacher's relationships with parents. For instance, some parents may think that the school's values conflict with their own values, or they may be intimidated by schools. These parents might respond negatively toward your efforts to develop relationships with them. Some parents will be interested in developing relationships with teachers and will be available to help out in the gymnasium. Other parents may want to be involved, but they may be unable to do so as a result of their busy schedules.

Steps for Getting to Know Parents

You can take several steps to help develop relationships with students' parents. First, you should try to establish positive relationships with your students' parents early in the year. For example, consider sending parents an e-mail to introduce yourself in early September. Parents who do not have e-mail access should be contacted via phone. Although this may take some time, contacting parents in this way will make it easier to deal with any problems that arise with a student at a later date.

Second, at the start of the school year, be sure to send home a beginning-of-school letter to each household, welcoming students and outlining your expectations for your physical education program. This letter should contain information about classroom routines and rules, as well as procedures regarding absences, homework, and assessment. Have parents sign and return this letter so you have a record that they have read and understand the contents of the letter. Resources 9.1 and 9.2 are examples of beginning-of-school letters for elementary and secondary levels respectively. If you are interested in having parents involved in activities in the gym, this letter is an excellent opportunity to list ways that parents can get involved. The following list provides examples of how parents can volunteer in physical education.

- ▶ Assist with fitness testing
- ▶ Assist with teaching skills (e.g., throwing, catching, jumping rope) to children who are struggling with those skills
- ▶ Help edit the physical education newsletter
- ▶ Write an article for the physical education newsletter
- ▶ Assist with a Jump Rope for Heart or Hoops for Heart event
- ▶ Assist with field days
- ▶ Chaperone field trips off campus (e.g., bowling alleys, climbing centers)
- ▶ Assist with before- and after-school activities such as before-school physical education and intramurals

Invite parents to call or e-mail you at school with any questions or concerns that they may have. Furthermore, as part of the beginning-of-school letter, you can include a survey that will help you gain valuable information about students. Resource 9.3 is a sample of a survey that could be sent as part of the beginning-of-school letter.

Next, open houses or back-to-school nights are excellent opportunities to develop relationships with parents. In most schools, your first formal introduction to parents will be in some form of an open house. To prepare, you should talk with your colleagues about ideas for topics to include in this session. Traditionally, open houses are a schoolwide event. Teachers share their academic programs, expectations, discipline policies, and any other pertinent information about their respective programs.

Make sure you thoroughly prepare for an open house and have an agenda for the evening. An agenda should include information regarding the curriculum and goals for the program, such as the philosophy of physical education, areas of curricular focus at certain grade levels, and assessment methods. In addition, discuss policies for areas such as discipline, grading, homework, and making up missed classes. Furthermore, let parents know that you will communicate with them throughout the year and that they are welcome to contact you. Finally, if you are seeking help with projects in physical education (i.e., fitness testing, field trips, and so on), the open house is a good opportunity to recruit volunteers.

A monthly or quarterly newsletter is another important tool for keeping parents abreast of what curricular units the students are participating in as well as information regarding assessment and out-of-school opportunities for physical activity. The possibilities are unlimited for the content of a newsletter. For example, a newsletter could include pictures of students participating in physical education, quotes from students about what they are learning in physical education, and even student articles about physical education. As part of the newsletter, you could also provide tips for parents who want to be active with their children as well as helpful websites and books that provide valuable information to parents regarding nutrition and physical activity. This newsletter could be available in hard copy or posted on the school's physical education website.

Physical education showcase nights are another great way to build relationships with parents. They are used to highlight what is special in your physical education program. These nights consist of students performing a variety of activities for their families and friends. Often these nights are organized around particular activities or grade levels. Although these nights are common at the elementary level, they can also be used with great success at the middle school and high school levels.

Finally, physical education "family fun nights" are also popular. On these nights, parents and family members can participate in physical education activities with their child. Activities that students and their families participate in on these nights could include a variety of station activities or specific activities such as dance.

▶ Parent volunteers can help with your physical education classes in many ways, including accompanying students on field trips.

Communicating With Parents

As a teacher, you can use several methods to communicate with parents. You need to stay in contact with them throughout the year. At times this can be overwhelming because of the sheer number of students that you deal with on a daily basis, but with some planning it is possible. You can contact parents during the school year using e-mail, phone calls, parent–teacher conferences, progress reports, report cards, postcards, and home visits. Home visits can be time consuming and somewhat unpredictable; however, visits to a student's home (with parents' prior approval) show that you care and may allow you to gain information that might not be accessible in any other way.

Be sure to contact parents when their child has done well or shown improvement, in addition to when there is a problem with the child. Parents often dread contacts from teachers because this usually signals that their child has done something wrong; however, parents are much more receptive to teacher contacts if the teacher also makes a point of sharing positive news about their child throughout the year. Resource 9.4 is an example of a "Caught Doing Something Good in Physical Education Report" that can be sent home throughout the year.

Communication is one of the most important skills for a teacher. No matter how much preparation, training, or experience you have, if you cannot communicate effectively with parents and students, you will not be successful as a teacher. Generally, it is best to communicate with parents via the telephone. Remember, parents need to believe that their concerns are important to teachers. You must listen and make parents feel that they are heard so that they will be more apt to work with you on behalf of their child. Take some time to think about what you want to say to the parent before you make the phone call. You should consider the following questions before making a phone call to a parent:

▶ What time should you call? Many parents work, and it may be easier to reach them outside of school hours.

▶ How will you begin the call? Be conversational and put the parent at ease with a friendly voice.

▶ What do you want to say in the conversation? Make notes before you make the call to keep the conversation focused.

▶ How will you end the conversation? Repeat the main points of the call, come to some agreement, and plan to follow up with the parent.

Throughout the phone call, you should take notes about what both you and the parent say. Document any parent contacts you have throughout the school year. If you decide during the phone call that you would like to set up a conference with the parent, ask the parent if he or she would be able to make arrangements to meet with you.

In addition to phone calls, formal communication can also be in the form of a letter printed on school letterhead. Any letter that is sent home should be proofread by a colleague. The letter must be professional and grammatically correct because parents expect that level of professionalism from a teacher. In the letter, you need to clearly state the purpose of your letter as well as your concerns. Additionally, parents who are not English speakers must receive the information in the letter in their primary language. School districts often employ translators to help with the translation of information contained in letters. For a letter going out to the parents of all your students who speak either English or a specific primary language such as Spanish, it is a good idea to print the letter in English on one side of the paper and in Spanish on the other.

E-mail is a popular and efficient way for teachers to communicate with parents; however, the best strategy is to use e-mail only to report positive information to parents about their children. E-mail messages can often be misinterpreted and result in feelings of ill will and conflict. For example, parents may have a question regarding why their child did not receive a good grade in physical education. If you respond via e-mail by simply stating that their child did not meet the course objectives, the parents may be upset with the lack of detail in your response as well as its brevity. The response, although it is correct, may result in the parents becoming confrontational with you and possibly contacting your principal. A more prudent response would be to express to the parents that you appreciate their concern and then ask them for a good time that you can contact them via telephone. Moreover, a parent may send you an e-mail that makes you angry, and your first reaction might be to send a hasty e-mail in response; however, it is often prudent to back away from the keyboard and telephone the parent.

Conducting Parent–Teacher Conferences

Parent–teacher conferences are a great opportunity to communicate with parents; however, parents often do not visit the physical education teacher on parent–teacher conference days. Sometimes parents do not make a point to visit the physical education teacher because they do not value physical education. In addition, the parents may only have a short amount of time to meet with their child's teachers, and they may deem it more important to meet with teachers who teach more "academic" subjects (at the secondary level) or the classroom teacher (at the elementary level). You should make appointments to meet with parents on these days, and you should also be available to parents who just stop by to see you on conference days. If some parents do not

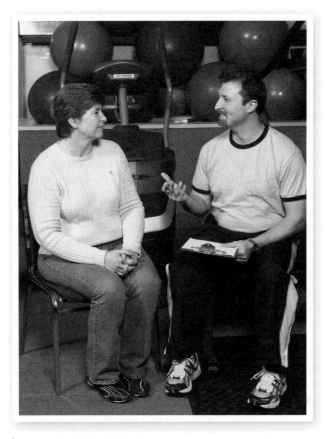

▶ Your parent–teacher conference will be more productive if you make the parent feel comfortable and talk about the student's strengths as well as any concerns.

speak English, arrange for an interpreter to attend the conference. If an interpreter is not available, perhaps the parent can bring a friend or another family member to translate.

If you are a physical education teacher at the elementary level, you should schedule your parent–teacher conferences with the classroom teacher (if the classroom teacher agrees to the arrangement). This way, parents meet with both you and the classroom teacher at the same time. Often, classroom teachers welcome the physical education teacher to these conferences, because the physical education teacher can provide information about the child in a context outside of the classroom setting.

Although parent–teacher conference days are beneficial for meeting with parents, you will also need to schedule conferences with parents at other times during the year. To do so, you will need to call the parents and set up an appointment for the conference. During that phone call, you should inform the parents that you will be sending them a letter before the conference in order to provide some details about the meeting and to gather essential information from them that may be beneficial to the conference. Resource 9.5 shows a sample letter that could be sent home before a conference.

Begin the conference by asking the parents about their day and by thanking them for coming. Allow them to express their interests and concerns about their child's education. Ask the parents for their perceptions of their child's strengths and weaknesses in physical education. You want the parents to feel welcome and comfortable at the conference. Allowing them to speak about their child's strengths first will help put them at ease.

Next, use the coaching feedback sandwich technique with the parents. This technique involves discussing with parents the student's strengths, followed by any concerns you have, and then wrapping it up by emphasizing the student's strengths once again. Be prepared to offer ideas to parents regarding how you and they might address your concerns. For example, if a student needs to participate more in activities outside of the school day to improve his skills and fitness, you could prepare a list of community resources, programs, and websites that may be helpful. Many parents are unaware of the variety of enrichment opportunities available in physical education.

End the conference in an upbeat manner. Thank the parents for their time and invite each person to summarize his or her understanding of the conference. Invite them to contact you with any further concerns. In addition, make plans for further communication regarding the progress of their child, whether by telephone, letter, e-mail, or another conference. Reemphasize any agreements or decisions made regarding the student. Write them down and give a copy to the parents. After the conference, write notes and reflect on what transpired in the conference. Resource 9.6 provides an example of a note-taking form that can be used for parent–teacher conferences.

Summary

Parents and guardians can be great allies to you. In light of this, you must make every attempt to develop relationships with parents and guardians, and you must communicate with them on a fairly regular basis. You can take several steps to develop relationships with parents, such as sending home a beginning-of-school letter, conducting an open house or physical education showcase night, producing a monthly or quarterly newsletter, and conducting a family fun night.

Furthermore, you can develop relationships with parents and guardians by effectively communicating with them. You can use several methods to communicate with parents or guardians, including e-mail, phone calls, notes or postcards home, and parent–teacher conferences.

DISCUSSION QUESTIONS

1. What actions would you take to develop relationships with parents?

2. Why is it important to communicate effectively with parents and guardians?

3. Why is e-mail communication not always the best type of communication?

Sample Beginning-of-School Letter to Parents (Elementary School)

Date: _____

Dear Parents or Guardians:

Hello, and welcome to a new school year at _____ Elementary School. I am very excited about the new school year, and I hope your child is also excited. I encourage you to examine the school's physical education website, which can be found at www._____. This website includes important information regarding the schedule for physical education as well as detailed information regarding policies and procedures in physical education.

Please make sure that your child brings appropriate clothes and tennis shoes on the days that he or she has physical education. In addition, please make sure that your child's shoes and clothes for physical education are clearly marked with your child's name.

Students will be expected to follow the classroom rules in physical education. The rules in physical education are (a) use positive language, (b) be respectful, and (c) demonstrate good sporting behavior. I will discuss these rules in detail with students the first day of physical education and will continue to reinforce them throughout the year.

Students will be assessed in a variety of ways in physical education. Students will be assessed on their skill development, their understanding of important physical education movement concepts, and their social skills in physical education.

I am looking forward to getting to know you and your child better. Please make every effort to attend the Open House on _____ at _____ p.m. If you have any questions before then, please feel free to call the school at _____ or e-mail me at _____. I will respond as soon as possible.

I am looking forward to a great year and a lot of fun and learning in physical education. I will see you at the Open House on _____.

Sincerely,

[Name]

Elementary physical education teacher

[Name of elementary school]

Please sign and return to school as soon as possible.

Print parent or guardian name: _____

Parent or guardian signature: _____

Date: _____

Sample Beginning-of-School Letter to Parents (High School)

Date: _____

Dear Parents or Guardians:

Welcome to a new school year at _____ High School. I am very excited to be teaching physical education to your child this year. Your child will participate in a variety of physical education units this year, including snowboarding, kayaking, and adventure challenge. I encourage you to view the school's physical education website (www._____) for a detailed description of the physical education curriculum as well as a description of policies and procedures related to physical education.

Your child is expected to dress for physical education and to be on time for class. Appropriate dress for physical education includes shorts or sweatpants, plain blue T-shirt, and athletic shoes. Shorts should be of an appropriate length. Students who do not dress for physical education are allowed to make up two days of physical education per quarter by attending physical education activities that are offered after school. Students are expected to make arrangements and obtain the proper documentation when making up the physical education class.

The physical education grade is part of the overall student grade point average; hence, I want to explain how students will be graded in physical education. Students will receive a letter grade for each unit that is taught in physical education. A specific percentage of the grade for each unit will be derived from students' skill, cognitive understanding, and social interactions with others.

On occasion, there will be homework for physical education. It is important that your child completes and returns physical education homework because it will have an impact on his or her grade for that unit of instruction.

I am looking forward to getting to know you and your child better. Please make every effort to attend the Open House on _____ at _____ p.m. If you have any questions before then, please feel free to call the school at _____ and leave a message. I will return your call as soon as possible.

Sincerely,

[Name]

Physical education teacher

[Name of high school]

Please sign and have your child return this letter to me at the next physical education class.

Print parent or guardian name: _____

Parent or guardian signature: _____

Date: _____

Survey to Be Included in Beginning-of-School Letter

Please complete this survey about your child. This information will help me get to know your child and meet your child's needs in physical education.

Name: _____

Nickname: _____

Address: _____

Telephone: _____

Birthday: _____

Medical conditions, including allergies: _____

_____

_____

Medications: _____

_____

Your child's favorite sports and physical activities: _____

_____

_____

Your child's hobbies and interests: _____

_____

_____

Your child's least favorite sports and physical activities: _____

_____

_____

Concerns you have about your child in physical education: _____

_____

_____

From A. James, 2013, *Survive and thrive as a physical educator: Strategies for the first year and beyond* (Champaign, IL: Human Kinetics).

Caught Doing Something Good in Physical Education Report

Dear Parents or Guardians:

This report is to inform you that your child was caught doing something good in physical education!

Your child is a super student in physical education because of the following:

_____ He or she is a great sport and values teamwork and playing more than winning.

_____ He or she encourages and compliments other students during physical education.

_____ He or she helps others to improve their skills.

_____ He or she is a positive role model.

_____ He or she listens and follows directions well.

_____ He or she cooperates with other students.

_____ Other: _____

_____

_____

I love having your child in my physical education class. He or she brightens my day and makes me appreciate my job as a teacher. Thank you for being such a wonderful parent and setting a great example for your child to follow. If you would like to discuss anything about your child, please contact me at school.

Sincerely,

[Name]

Physical education teacher

[School name]

From A. James, 2013, *Survive and thrive as a physical educator: Strategies for the first year and beyond* (Champaign, IL: Human Kinetics).

Sample Parent–Teacher Conference Letter

Date: _____

Dear Parents:

Next week, on _____, you and I will meet and talk about the progress of your child in physical education. I am excited to share information with you regarding your child's progress in physical education.

When we meet, I will be talking about the following:

1. What we are doing in physical education and what my expectations are for all students

2. Your child's strengths in physical education as well as anything that your child may need to work on

3. How you and I can work together to help your child get the most out of physical education and become a physically educated individual

4. Anything you would like to talk about

Because of the limited time we have scheduled, it would help if I knew what questions and concerns you have ahead of time. Please use the space below to jot down any questions and concerns that you might have. Please send these back to school with your child or bring them to the conference.

Questions I have:

_____

_____

_____

Thank you for your time. I look forward to meeting with you.

Sincerely,

[Name]

Physical education teacher

[Name of school]

From A. James, 2013, *Survive and thrive as a physical educator: Strategies for the first year and beyond* (Champaign, IL: Human Kinetics).

Parent–Teacher Conference Note-Taking Form

Student:_____

Date: _____

Main discussion points in the conference:

Strategies to try with the student:

Means of follow-up with the parent:

Teacher signature:_____

Date: _____

Parent signature: _____

Date: _____

From A. James, 2013, *Survive and thrive as a physical educator: Strategies for the first year and beyond* (Champaign, IL: Human Kinetics).

CHAPTER 10

Professional Development

Professional development is important for all teachers. You would be mistaken to believe that your college education will teach you everything you need to know to be an effective physical education teacher. In fact, the journey of a beginning teacher is just commencing at college graduation.

A big piece of this journey is professional development, which will help you grow as an educator. Professional development is important for several reasons. First, professional development can enhance your effectiveness as a teacher and lead to more job satisfaction. Second, engaging in professional development activities will help you remain enthusiastic about teaching physical education and avoid experiencing burnout. You can explore several options that will enhance your professional and personal growth as a teacher, including the following: joining professional organizations, reading professional literature, continuing your education, creating a professional development plan and portfolio, and working with a mentor.

Professional Organizations

Throughout your college experience, professors probably encouraged you to join your state and national professional organization. You may have done so as a student, but now as a teacher, you may question the value of that professional membership. Although a professional membership costs more than a student membership, the cost is worth it in terms of member benefits.

The national professional organization for physical education is the American Alliance for Health, Physical Education, Recreation and Dance (AAHPERD). AAHPERD is an organization that is composed of six associations:

- ▶ American Association for Health Education
- ▶ American Association for Physical Activity and Recreation
- ▶ National Association for Girls and Women in Sport
- ▶ National Association for Sport and Physical Education
- ▶ National Dance Association
- ▶ Research Consortium

In addition to the six associations, the structure of AAHPERD also includes six districts: Eastern, Central, Midwest, Southern, Southwest, and Northwest (figure 10.1). The districts cover different geographic regions of the United States. AAHPERD members in states that fall within each district make up the membership of that district.

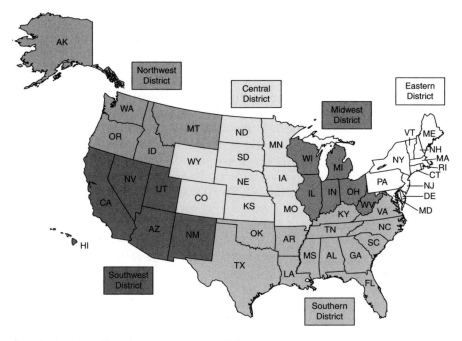

▶ **FIGURE 10.1**   The six districts of AAHPERD.

Membership in AAHPERD provides several member benefits, including professional development opportunities and advocacy for physical education. Members also receive full access to a website (www.aahperd.org) that offers information and downloadable forms and tools for teachers as well as literature that helps teachers stay abreast of current topics in physical education.

One of the most significant professional development opportunities that AAHPERD provides is national and district conferences. The national AAHPERD conference is held once a year. In addition, most districts hold district conferences once a year. These conferences offer several sessions that provide ideas for enhancing instruction as well as opportunities to network with professionals who truly care about teaching physical education. By attending these conferences, you have the opportunity to present your ideas and activities. Presenting at conferences is a very good professional development opportunity. It allows you to share ideas and receive feedback from peers that can further enhance your professional growth and effectiveness as a teacher.

In addition to the conferences, AAHPERD offers a number of professional development workshops throughout the country. These include workshops that are based on national standards and best practices. Examples of these workshops include active gaming and interactive fitness workshops, curriculum development workshops, and workshops regarding the use of technology in physical education. In addition to these workshops, AAHPERD offers Physical Best workshops and a coaching educators' conference. Furthermore, the American Association for Physical Activity and Recreation offers a variety of workshops in adapted physical education, fitness, and recreation.

Advocacy is another important benefit that is offered by AAHPERD. Although most teachers would like to be able to go to Washington to lobby for physical education, the reality is that they are seldom able to do so as a result of their teaching schedule. AAHPERD works to promote physical education and physical activity by lobbying and educating members of the legislative branch about the importance of these topics and by focusing on specific legislative priorities. For example, AAHPERD is involved in supporting the reauthorization of the Elementary and Secondary Education Act (ESEA). AAHPERD is also involved in supporting legislation to make physical education and health education core subjects and supporting PEP (Carol M. White) grant funding. In addition, members of AAHPERD have the opportunity to get involved and support legislation through links provided on the AAHPERD website.

Membership in AAHPERD entitles a teacher to receive one of four journals:

▶ *The Journal of Physical Education, Recreation and Dance (JOPERD)*
▶ *Strategies*
▶ *Research Quarterly for Exercise and Science (RQES)*
▶ *American Journal of Health Education (AJHE)*

JOPERD and *Strategies* are teacher-oriented journals that contain valuable articles as well as interesting tips and activities that are of interest to physical educators. *RQES* is a journal that publishes research articles. This journal includes a pedagogy (teaching) section that highlights pedagogical research as well as other sections that focus on research in other areas of exercise and sport. The *American Journal of Health Education* is a journal that contains articles that would be of interest to health educators and other people who are concerned about health promotion. In addition, AAHPERD publishes newsletters throughout the year. Each member receives *Update PLUS,* which is published six times per year. It contains a variety of articles on topics such as career development and financial planning.

Many teachers do not take the time to read professional literature; however, this literature is a valuable resource for teachers. In my experience, I have found that the best way to read professional literature is to schedule 20 to 30 minutes into my day to read articles of interest. Sometimes I break the 20 to 30 minutes up into two or three 10-minute reading sessions. Even then, this gives me enough time to read and stay abreast of what is happening in the field and to reflect on how I can change my teaching practice for the better.

In addition to joining AAHPERD, you should also be a member of your state AHPERD. This allows you to be professionally involved at a local level. State AHPERDs provide member benefits that are similar but not as extensive as those provided by AAHPERD. For example, many state AHPERDs hold state conventions, publish newsletters at regular intervals, and advocate for physical education within the state. In addition, several state AHPERDs have been instrumental in supporting initiatives such as the creation and implementation of state physical education standards and statewide assessment in physical education.

You have opportunities to take on leadership roles within AAHPERD and your state AHPERD. For example, the New York State Association for Health, Physical Education, Recreation and Dance (NYSAHPERD) has several educators on the Executive Council and Board of Directors. These educators have taken on leadership positions to create change in physical education in New York. They frequently comment that their service to NYSAHPERD has contributed significantly to their professional growth and development as teachers. For example, Jason Lehmbeck, a past president of NYSAHPERD stated, "My work with NYSAHPERD charges my batteries and reenergizes me to continue to teach physical education" (NYSAHPERD Executive Council Meeting, summer 2009).

▶ Meeting with other physical education teachers to discuss outcomes and strategies can help you learn new skills and further your professional development.

In addition, Lonnie Wilson, a member of the NYSAHPERD Executive Council communicated the value of being involved with her state association in the following statement: "My affiliation with NYSAHPERD has been invaluable to me. The people that I have had the honor to work with over the years have helped to shape me, motivate me and ignite my passion for health, physical education and lifelong fitness" (L. Wilson, personal communication, January 5, 2012).

Getting involved with your national and state AHPERD will help you continue to develop as a professional. It will also help you stay passionate about teaching and learning in physical education. Through your involvement with these organizations, you will be able to network with individuals who support high-quality physical education as well as enhance your effectiveness as an educator.

Continuing Your Education

Several other opportunities are available that will enable you to enhance your professional development. One is to continue your education. A professor once told me that one way to stay enthused about teaching is to always keep learning and to never think that I know everything there is to know about teaching physical education. I have never forgotten this advice, and throughout my career, I have sought opportunities to learn more about teaching physical education.

Many teachers return to a university or college to obtain a master's degree. Several states require a master's degree to receive a "professional" teaching certification in that state; however, requirements for each state vary. Check the website of your state's department of education to determine requirements that are specific to the state in which you teach. Teachers today have several options in pursuing their graduate studies, including online and hybrid programs. Hybrid programs are programs that include classes that may meet a few times on campus; however, most of the instruction is online. As a result of technology, many students do not have to travel to a college or university to pursue their studies. Currently, some graduate programs are offered completely online. The convenience of online graduate programs allows you to gain experience teaching while pursuing your degree at the same time.

Graduate study in physical education can enhance your knowledge and skills in many ways. For example, you will learn a great deal about instructional approaches and developing meaningful curriculums that can make physical education more significant to your students. In addition, you can enhance your ability to read and understand research as well as begin to make connections between research findings and your own teaching of physical education.

Professional Development Plan

You need to create a professional development plan. This plan serves as a guide to help you plot a course for professional development throughout your teaching career. It is a very useful tool that will help you work toward professional goals and become an effective teacher.

Professional development goals are an important part of the professional development plan. Professional development goals should be set in the beginning of the academic year. To become an effective physical education teacher, you need to make a commitment to specific goals that will help you become more successful. For example, perhaps you would like to increase your content knowledge, attend a conference, or possibly read professional literature such as *JOPERD*.

Meeting professional goals may be difficult for you because you may not know how to set these goals. In addition, your district may have specific professional development requirements and may dictate when and where professional development will occur. District-sponsored professional development activities often focus on very general aspects of teaching and may not meet your specific professional development needs.

Professional development goals can be short or long term. Short-term goals can be achieved in a relatively brief amount of time. These goals focus on immediately useful tasks or teaching strategies. For example, a short-term goal may be to incorporate more fitness-producing activities into the curriculum. Short-term goals also reinforce the significance of setting goals, build confidence to undertake more challenging goals, and often lead directly to long-term goals, some of which will guide professional development activities for years to come (Boreen, Johnson, Niday, & Potts, 2009).

Long-term goals reach beyond the immediate concerns of the gymnasium and may lead to improved instructional performance. Unlike short-term goals, these goals are developed with a vision of the future. For example, a long-term goal may be to get a master's degree. Long-term goals form an integral part of your professional development plan.

Another piece of the professional development plan is to decide which professional development activities you will undertake to achieve your professional goals. For example, perhaps your goal is to become well versed in using assessment to enhance the teaching-learning process in your classroom; in this case, you may choose to attend a state AHPERD conference to learn more about assessment. You must identify professional development activities that will help you reach your goals. Resource 10.1 provides a template for developing short-term goals for a professional development plan. Resource 10.2 is a template for creating long-term goals.

▶ Consider recording one of your class sessions so that you can analyze your own teaching performance and identify potential areas for improvement.

Professional Development Teaching Portfolio

One way to evaluate success in reaching professional goals is through the creation and use of a professional development teaching portfolio. This portfolio provides a place to house your professional development plan; documentation of professional development activities and teaching practices; artifacts such as unit plans, lesson plans, and assessments; and reflections regarding progress toward professional development goals. Reflecting on the artifacts included in your portfolio will help you make progress toward your professional goals. Through this reflection, you can deepen your understanding of your values and beliefs about teaching and learning. The following examples of artifacts could be included in a professional development teaching portfolio.

▶ Professional development plan with short- and long-term goals
▶ A list of professional development activities with a short reflection about how each activity contributed to meeting your short- and long-term goals and enhanced your teaching effectiveness

▶ Honors and distinctions (awards, lists of achievements such as conference presentations, honorary societies)

▶ Sample unit plans

▶ Sample lesson plans

▶ Sample assessments

▶ Samples of student work with your written feedback and evaluation

▶ Written observations completed by administrators or peers

▶ Videotape of your teaching

▶ Letters of recommendation

▶ Resume

Mentors

Mentors play a large role in your success. Typically, you will be assigned a mentor; however, you should seek out a mentor if you are not assigned one. The best mentor is a colleague in your school or district who has an in-depth understanding of students in the district as well as district and school politics. An effective mentor, combined with engagement in other professional development activities, can help you avoid the washout effect described in chapter 8.

Your mentor does not have to be a physical education teacher; however, being a physical education teacher may make the mentor more effective. A mentor who is a physical education teacher may be more prepared to help you develop teaching skills related to physical education than someone who has not been trained as a physical educator.

Mentors are essential in helping you overcome the feelings of insecurity that may arise if the reality of teaching is different from your expectations. You may experience reality shock (as described in chapter 8) because of a gap between your preparation and the requirements of the job. Mentors are critical in helping you deal with the effects of reality shock. Mentors provide support and help you maintain a level of motivation for teaching without becoming disillusioned with the challenges that come with teaching physical education.

In addition, mentors will be vital in helping you understand and confront challenging workplace conditions. For example, a mentor may need to assist you with strategies for meeting the needs of diverse learners, addressing the lack of collaboration with colleagues, or dealing with poor resources and school conditions. In addition, mentors are essential in integrating you into the school culture. They can assist you in learning the culture of the school as well as the organizational and political system of the school. Furthermore, they can provide you with strategies to help you successfully navigate through the school culture and political system.

Summary

Professional development in physical education is essential for you to continue to develop as an educator. In addition, you can enhance your effectiveness as a teacher through numerous professional development activities. Some of these activities include joining professional organizations (such as AAHPERD and your state AHPERD), reading professional literature, continuing your education, creating a professional development plan, and getting guidance from a mentor.

Joining a professional organization has many benefits that will enhance your professional development. For example, AAHPERD and state AHPERDs offer annual conferences and workshops that provide excellent opportunities for professional development. Attending these events is a great way to increase your knowledge base about teaching physical education.

Another professional development activity you can undertake is to create a professional development plan. This plan serves as a road map for professional development throughout your career. You should review the plan and reflect on your progress toward meeting professional development goals.

Having a mentor will also enhance your professional development. A mentor can provide a great deal of insight into the politics and structure of the school. In addition, a mentor can assist you with many of the day-to-day issues that you will encounter as a teacher.

DISCUSSION QUESTIONS

1. Why is professional development important throughout your career?

2. What professional development activities do you believe are the most important? Why?

3. What are your short- and long-term goals for professional development?

4. What professional development activities will you undertake to accomplish your professional development goals?

Graphic Organizer for Short-Term Goal Setting

Name: _____

Short-term goals	Activities to help accomplish goals	Date goals were accomplished

From A. James, 2013, *Survive and thrive as a physical educator: Strategies for the first year and beyond* (Champaign, IL: Human Kinetics).

Graphic Organizer for Long-Term Goal Setting

Name: _____

Long-term goals	Activities to help accomplish goals	Date goals were accomplished

Appendix A

Frequently Asked Questions

Over the years, I have been asked many questions by new teachers. In this appendix, I have compiled some of the most frequently asked questions. Most of these questions are related to content within the book; when appropriate, I point readers to chapters that may have more information.

1. Is Detailed Planning Necessary?

Planning is essential for student learning and effective instruction. Typically, the more experience you gain as a teacher, the less dependent you will be on a plan; however, you will still need to plan. Many veteran teachers keep binders that contain units, lesson plans, and assessments they have planned in the past. They use this material as a basis for units of instruction that they are currently planning. More information on planning can be found in chapter 3.

2. What Kind of Assessment Should I Use?

Teachers have several types of assessments at their disposal. Chapter 4 contains information on various types of assessments. The important thing to remember is that the assessments need to align with the objectives and learning activities in order to ensure instructional alignment. Units and lessons that are instructionally aligned lead to more student learning.

3. How Should I Establish a Grading Policy?

Check with your administrator or the school handbook to determine if there are any school policies about grading. In addition, discuss policies with your colleagues. Base your grading policy on the three domains: psychomotor, cognitive, and affective. For each domain, assign a percentage that will weight the domain relative to the emphasis to be placed on each domain in your grading philosophy—for example, 50 percent on the psychomotor domain, 30 percent on the cognitive domain, and 20 percent on the affective domain. Information regarding the establishment of a grading policy can be found in chapter 4.

4. How Should I Compute a Grade?

Grades can be computed in several ways. You need to make a plan at the beginning of the year for how you will handle this task. If you like, you can speak with colleagues about their approaches; however, you must ensure that the grade is based on student learning—not effort, participation, or being prepared. Refer to chapter 4 for detailed information regarding how to compute a grade.

5. How Do I Encourage Students to Complete Homework?

You need to create a culture in the gymnasium that values homework, and you must make sure that students realize that homework is an important aspect of physical education. In addition, homework must be a regular part of physical education, not something that is done once a year. Teachers can make homework more exciting by involving families in the homework. For example, have the student perform some type of physical activity with a family member; ask the student to log the activity and have the parent sign off on the activity. Furthermore, the student could interview family members about what they like or do not like about physical activity and how they could be more physically active.

6. What Should I Do if Students Do Not Return Physical Education Homework?

Students may not bring in their physical education homework because they do not believe that it is important. A teacher needs to build a culture that values all types of assessment, including homework. One way to make homework valuable to students is to link it to their grade. While collecting homework, emphasize the importance of homework and how it helps students learn. In addition, find a way to acknowledge students who turn homework in on time. You should also correct homework promptly and discuss it briefly in class.

7. How Do I Incorporate Technology Into My Program?

You can incorporate several types of technology into your program, including computers, heart rate monitors, pedometers, game bikes, accelerometers, video cameras, and digital cameras. Students today are very tech savvy and enjoy the use of technology in physical education. Many teachers use the Internet to search for lesson and assessment ideas; however, you should be careful because some ideas found online are good while others are not. Information about using technology to motivate students can be found in chapter 6.

8. What Should I Do if I Suspect That a Student Is a Victim of Physical or Mental Abuse?

You must know the procedure for your school or district. You are required by law to report any suspicion of abuse. Also speak with support staff such as school counselors, psychologists, social workers, or other community resource people who work with your students. These individuals will provide you with assistance and guidance.

9. Should I Try to Be a Friend to My Students?

The answer is absolutely no. You are the teacher, which means that you are the adult who is responsible for student well-being and student learning. Students will consider you as an equal if you try to be their friend. Teachers who make the mistake of trying to be a friend to their students have trouble maintaining classroom discipline and find it difficult to instruct students in a manner that enhances student learning.

10. How Do I Help a Student Whose First Language Is Not English?

One thing that a teacher can do is to pair the student with a "buddy" who may or may not speak the primary language of the student. Of course, it will be a better pairing if the student does speak the primary language of the other student. In addition, when giving directions, make sure you speak clearly with understandable language. Effective demonstrations are also important. Chapter 7 offers more information about teaching students whose first language is not English.

11. What Should I Put on Bulletin Boards?

Bulletin boards are a great instructional tool. You should use a bulletin board to post information related to the units that you are currently teaching. The bulletin board can also be used to display information about community resources that are available to students. This will encourage students to participate in physical activities outside of school, including the activities that they are learning in physical education.

12. How Do I Prepare for a Substitute Teacher?

Put together a substitute folder that includes class rosters, class routines and rules, duties that the substitute has to cover for you, and your teaching schedule. Include several activities that your students enjoy; these activities should be connected to the unit that you are teaching at the time. Find a colleague who is willing to check in with the sub and provide any assistance that the sub may need. Ask the substitute to leave you notes regarding how the day went. Chapter 2 provides more details about preparing for a substitute teacher.

13. How Do I Prepare Students to Behave for a Sub?

Be sure to speak with students about what is expected of them if you ever have to be absent and a substitute teacher fills in. Explain to students that the substitute is a teacher just like you are. Tell the students that they should make the teacher feel welcome and should demonstrate the same respect for the substitute that they show for you. When you return, make it a point to congratulate students on their behavior and the positive comments that you received from the substitute teacher.

14. How Do I Prepare Students for a Field Trip?

Students in physical education often go on field trips to off-campus sites. These sites may include the local bowling alley, an ice rink, or a local park. You must communicate to students what you expect from them while they are on a field trip. Be very specific about your expectations and provide concrete examples of these expectations during the discussion.

15. What Should I Do if Students Are Slow to Transition From Task to Task?

You need to hold students accountable for moving efficiently from one task to another. A concrete transition routine is necessary for efficient transitions. One transition routine is to say, "When I say go, you have 5 seconds to do _____ and then come sit at home base. One, two, three . . ." After the transition, thank students for moving quickly. Information about transitions and the importance of stating transitions in a complete manner can be found in chapter 5.

16. What Should I Do When Students Do Not Want to Participate?

Students who do not want to participate have probably not experienced a lot of success in physical education. Keeping this in mind, you must try to convince these students that they can succeed. Provide these students with tasks in which they can be successful and praise them regularly.

Another reason that students may not want to participate is because they find the activities boring. Provide tasks that are meaningful as well as challenging to students. Motivating students to participate is discussed in detail in chapter 6.

17. What Should I Do When Students Tattle?

Tattling is a very common behavior for young elementary students. You must distinguish the difference between tattling and telling. You should teach students to tell if someone is hurt or if someone is hurting them; however, students also need to be taught that tattling on someone who is doing something wrong—when it doesn't concern them—is not appropriate. As tattling decreases, praise students and let them know how proud you are of them that they are able to take care of themselves.

18. What Should I Do When Students Talk While I Am Presenting a Lesson?

You can do several things to get students' attention while you are presenting a lesson. For example, you can simply say the names of the students who are talking. In addition, you can wait for quiet. Another effective technique with elementary students is to point out students who are listening. You should point out more than one student at a time. For example, you could say, "I really like the way Jim and DeMarcus are listening."

Students often talk if they think the lesson is boring or too difficult. With this in mind, you should design lessons that are exciting, maximize participation, and keep instruction to a minimum.

19. What Should I Do When a Student Talks Back to Me?

If students talk back to you, tell them that their behavior is inappropriate and that they are welcome to discuss their concerns with you during lunch or after school. If they continue to talk back, tell them that you are not willing to talk to them about it at this time and that you will speak with them when they can be respectful in the conversation.

20. What Can I Do to Gain the Respect of My Students?

Teachers today do not automatically get respect for being a teacher. Teachers can gain respect by developing positive relationships with students and by knowing and teaching their subject matter well. A teacher must be consistent with students and treat them with respect. More information about developing relationships with students and gaining their respect can be found in chapter 6.

21. How Do I Handle Students Who Bully Other Students?

As a teacher, you are expected to take all steps necessary to prevent bullying, including teaching students what bullying is and what you expect them to do if they see someone being bullied or if they themselves are bullied. You must act quickly when you see a student being bullied. Do not ignore the situation. Address the situation and document what happened. Follow the school's policy regarding bullying, and follow up with the administration and the parents or guardians. Be sure to inform parents or guardians to let them know what happened and how the incident is being addressed.

22. What Should I Do When Students Get Into a Fight?

You are expected to know and follow your school district's procedures for handling student fights. You should keep your students as safe as possible when a fight breaks out. You should take measures to stop fights without putting yourself or others in danger. For example, tell the students to stop, and send two students to get another adult to help. In addition, you must document what happened before, during, and after the fight in case there is litigation.

Avoid trying to physically restrain students from fighting. Teachers who try to stop a fight may get hurt or unintentionally injure the students who are fighting.

23. What Should I Do if the Entire Class Is Misbehaving and I Cannot Get Their Attention?

Anytime students are too loud or not listening, you need to get their attention. One way to get their attention is to have a specific signal. Obviously, a whistle can be used as a signal; however, there are other attention-getting signals that are efficient. For example, you may use a clap signal that is performed with a specific rhythm. Another attention-getting routine is to say, "If you can hear my voice, clap your hands one time." Follow this with "If you can hear my voice, clap two times," and so on, until all students are clapping and you have their attention.

24. How Can I Start Building Community in My Classes in the Gymnasium?

One thing that helps to build community in the gym is having a routine to follow at the beginning of each class. Greeting students as they come into the gym and checking in with them are a great way to convey to them that you are glad they are here and that they are an important member of the class. The use of a home base to conduct closure at the end of class can also help build community. Using a home base as a meeting place provides students with a specific location for the lesson closure as well as a place to discuss anything that students deem important. This is also a good way to address and collectively solve issues such as poor sporting behavior.

25. When Should I Call Parents About Student Misbehavior and What Should I Say?

You need to contact parents about unacceptable behavior. Always start the parent contact by saying something positive about their child. Early in the conversation, let the parents know that you are contacting them because you care about the student and want the student to do well. Explain to the parents what the child did that was inappropriate. Ask the parents if they know of anything that could be bothering the student that could have contributed to the behavior. Tell the parents about the action you plan to take and ask them for their input. Sometimes it is a good idea to come up with an action that involves the parents as well. For example, you could send home a daily progress report for the parent to sign and the child to return. More tips for communicating with parents can be found in chapter 9.

26. What Should I Do When a Parent Questions a Grade I Have Given?

Listen to the parents' concerns without interrupting and then calmly explain the basis for the grade. In addition, be sure to have documentation of how the grade was computed. For example, assessments in the three domains that were used to compute the grade as well as your overall grading plan will serve as valuable documentation to justify the grade.

27. What Are Some Ways I Can Start Building a Support System for Myself?

You need to develop networks of support within your profession. People in these networks will have similar experiences and will be able to understand your daily struggles. They will help you remain passionate about the teaching profession. Some people form a support group with other physical education colleagues, while others have support groups that include teachers from different academic disciplines. It is a good idea to combine socializing with support. Teachers often participate in athletic activities or go out to dinner to engage in discussion about issues in the gymnasium. Chapter 8 offers more information about building a personal support system.

28. What Is Tenure and How Does the Tenure Process Work?

Teacher tenure is basically a permanent job contract for a school teacher. Tenure is granted to teachers who have proven their teaching skills as well as facilitated student learning. In most cases, a teacher must work a certain number of years (typically 2 to 4 years) before becoming eligible to receive tenure. The granting of tenure is typically based on a teacher's annual performance review that is conducted by various administrators.

Appendix B

Resources

You will need a lot of resources to become a skilled teacher. In chapter 2, the importance of developing a professional library was discussed. This appendix provides resources that would be great additions to your professional library. The resources presented include only a sample of those that are available; however, they are some of the best resources for a beginning teacher to have. Each of them not only will help you to become a more skillful teacher but also will further your content knowledge about teaching physical education.

Websites

PHYSICAL EDUCATION AND COACHING WEBSITES

www.pecentral.org

PE Central is a website that provides information about developmentally appropriate physical education practices and programs.

www.aahperd.org

This is the website for AAHPERD, the professional organization whose mission is to promote and support healthy lifestyles through high-quality programs in physical education and health.

www.humankinetics.com

Human Kinetics is a publisher of numerous physical education, sports, and recreation resources, including books, e-books, DVDs, and apps.

www.sparkpe.org

Spark PE is a website that provides physical education materials that were created by a nonprofit organization of San Diego State University. This organization is committed to creating, implementing, and evaluating programs that promote lifelong wellness.

www.pe4life.org

PE4life is a website that advocates for improved fitness, social behavior, and learning readiness of children by educating schools and their community partners to be catalysts for change in advancing high-quality physical education.

www.pelinks4u.org

This website provides a monthly online magazine promoting active, health-enhancing lifestyles and success-oriented programs in health and physical education. The site has links for advocacy efforts, fundraising, and ideas for lesson and unit plans.

www.physicaleducationupdate.com

The Physical Education Update website contains links to physical education videos, activities, and information on topics such as sport science and nutrition.

www.heart.org

The American Heart Association website provides information relating to cardiovascular health as well as activities that focus on heart health and physical activity in general that can be taught in the gymnasium.

www.pa.org

The Project Adventure website provides information on adventure-based programming designed to develop responsible individuals through adventure activities.

www.cooperinstitute.org

The Cooper Institute website provides information regarding health and fitness education, physical activity research, and the Fitnessgram.

www.nhsca.com

The National High School Coaches Association website includes information regarding student-athletes, coaching certifications, and how to help student-athletes get into college.

www.nhsaca.org

The National High School Athletic Coaches Association website provides information regarding strength and conditioning for high school athletes, links to state coaching associations, and information on nutrition.

INSTRUCTIONAL OR TEACHING WEBSITES

www.rubristar4teachers.org

This website provides teachers with templates for creating rubrics.

www.puzzlemaker.com

The Puzzlemaker website allows the user to create various types of puzzles, including word searches.

www.certificatecreator.com

The Certificate Creator website allows the user to make and print certificates and awards.

www.teachnology.com

This website contains links to rubric makers, printable resources for teachers, and ideas for lesson plans in physical education.

www.atozteacherstuff.com

This website contains links to word search generators, ideas for lesson plans in physical education, and a discussion forum for teachers.

www.lessonplans.com

This website provides a link to several lesson plans that can be used in physical education.

www.teachervision.com

TeacherVision is a very comprehensive website. It contains links to physical education lesson plans, ideas and tips regarding classroom management and assessment, graphic organizers that will help students develop literacy skills (such as comparing and contrasting), and customizable awards and certificates.

www.free-clipart-pictures.net

This website provides free clip art. Teachers can find clip art related to sport and physical activity as well as other types of clip art that can be useful for physical education.

www.pureclipart.com

This website provides free clip art, including several categories of sport clip art that can be useful to physical education teachers.

www.testdesigner.com

The test designer website provides multiple-choice, true–false, fill-in-the-blank, and open-ended test questions that can be used to design a written test for many activities in physical education.

Books

Allison, P.C., & Barrett, K.R. (2000). *Constructing children's physical education experiences: Understanding the content for teaching.* Boston: Allyn and Bacon.

Belka, D.E. (1994). *Teaching children games: Becoming a master teacher.* Champaign, IL: Human Kinetics.

Buck, M.M., Lund, J.L., Harrison, J.M., & Cook, C.B. (2007). *Instructional strategies for secondary school physical education* (6th ed.). New York: McGraw-Hill.

Bulger, S.M., Mohr, D.J., Rairigh, R.M., & Townsend, J.S. (2006). *Sport education seasons: Featuring basketball, soccer and fitness education.* Champaign, IL: Human Kinetics.

Buschner, C.A. (1994). *Teaching children movement concepts and skills: Becoming a master teacher.* Champaign, IL: Human Kinetics.

Castelli, D.M., & Fiorentino, L.H. (2008). *Physical education technology playbook.* Champaign, IL: Human Kinetics.

Cone, T.P., & Cone, S.L. (2005). *Teaching children dance* (2nd ed.). Champaign, IL: Human Kinetics.

Cone, T.P., Werner, P., & Cone, S.L. (2009). *Interdisciplinary elementary physical education: Connecting, sharing, partnering* (2nd ed.). Champaign, IL: Human Kinetics.

Corbin, C.B., Corbin, W.R., Welk, G.J., & Welk, K.A. (2008). *Concepts of physical fitness: Active lifestyles for wellness* (14th ed.). New York: McGraw-Hill.

Darst, P.W., Pangrazi, R.P., Sariscony, M.J., & Brusseau, T.A. (2012). *Dynamic physical education for secondary school students* (7th ed.). San Francisco, CA: Benjamin Cummings.

Fronske, H.A. (2008). *Teaching cues for sport skills for secondary school students* (4th ed.). New York: Pearson/Benjamin Cummings.

Graham, G. (2008). *Teaching children physical education: Becoming a master teacher* (3rd ed.). Champaign, IL: Human Kinetics.

Graham, G., Holt/Hale, S.A., & Parker, M. (2010). *Children moving: A reflective approach to teaching physical education* (8th ed.). New York: McGraw-Hill.

Himberg, C., Hutchinson, G.E., & Roussell, J.M. (2003). *Teaching secondary physical education: Preparing adolescents to be active for life.* Champaign, IL: Human Kinetics.

Hopple, C.J. (2005). *Elementary physical education teaching and assessment: A practical guide* (2nd ed.). Champaign, IL: Human Kinetics.

Lund, J.L., & Kirk, M.F. (2010). *Performance-based assessment for middle and high school physical education* (2nd ed.). Champaign, IL: Human Kinetics.

Mitchell, S.A., Oslin, J.L., & Griffin, L.L. (2003). *Sport foundations for elementary physical education: A tactical games approach.* Champaign, IL: Human Kinetics.

Mitchell, S.A., Oslin, J.L., & Griffin, L.L. (2006). *Teaching sport concepts and skills: A tactical games approach* (2nd ed.). Champaign, IL: Human Kinetics.

Mohnsen, B.S. (2008). *Teaching middle school physical education: A standards based approach for grades 5-8* (3rd ed.). Champaign, IL: Human Kinetics.

National Association for Sport and Physical Education. (2004). *Moving into the future: National standards for physical education* (2nd ed.). Reston, VA: Author.

National Association for Sport and Physical Education. (2005). *Physical Best activity guide: Elementary level* (2nd ed.). Champaign, IL: Human Kinetics.

National Association for Sport and Physical Education. (2005). *Physical Best activity guide: Middle and high school levels* (2nd ed.). Champaign, IL: Human Kinetics.

National Association for Sport and Physical Education. (2008). *PE metrics: Assessing the national standards: Standard 1: Elementary.* Reston, VA: Author.

National Association for Sport and Physical Education. (2011). *PE metrics: Assessing national standards 1-6 in secondary school.* Reston, VA: Author.

Ratliffe, T., & Ratliffe, L.M. (1994). *Teaching children fitness: Becoming a master teacher.* Champaign, IL: Human Kinetics.

Rink, J.E. (2010). *Teaching physical education for learning* (6th ed.). New York: McGraw-Hill.

Schiemer, S. (2000). *Assessment strategies for elementary physical education.* Champaign, IL: Human Kinetics.

Schmottlach, N., & McManama, J. (2006). *Physical education activity handbook* (11th ed.). New York: Pearson/Benjamin Cummings.

Siedentop, D., Hastie, P.A., & van der Mars, H. (2011). *Complete guide to sport education* (2nd ed.). Champaign, IL: Human Kinetics.

Siedentop, D., & Tannehill, D. (2000). *Developing teaching skills in physical education* (4th ed.). Mountain View, CA: Mayfield Publishing Company.

Werner, P.H. (1994). *Teaching children gymnastics: Becoming a master teacher.* Champaign, IL: Human Kinetics.

Periodicals

Journal of Physical Education, Recreation and Dance (Reston, VA: AAHPERD). Available from AAHPERD, 1900 Association Drive, Reston, Virginia 22091.

Provides articles on current issues and methods in physical education, athletics, recreation, and dance. Articles focus on both theory and practice.

Research Quarterly for Exercise and Science (Reston, VA: AAHPERD). Available from AAHPERD, 1900 Association Drive, Reston, Virginia 22091.

Provides research on exercise and sport that is reviewed by an editorial board.

Strategies (Reston, VA: AAHPERD). Available from AAHPERD, 1900 Association Drive, Reston, Virginia 22091.

Provides ideas and activities that can be used in elementary and secondary physical education classes.

Journal of Teaching in Physical Education (Champaign, IL: Human Kinetics). Available from Human Kinetics Publishers, Inc., P.O. Box 5076, Champaign, Illinois 61825-5076.

Provides research on teaching physical education that is reviewed by an editorial board.

Equipment Suppliers

Flaghouse, Inc.

150 N. MacQueen Pkway.
Mount Vernon, NY 10550
www.flaghouse.com

Gopher Sport

120 Oakdale St.
Owatonna, MN 55060
www.gophersport.com

Palos Sports, Inc.

12235 S. Harlem Ave.
Palos Heights, IL 60463
www.palossports.com

Sportime

One Sportime Way
Atlanta, GA 30340
www.sportime.com

References

AlMunajjed, M. (1997). *Women in Saudi Arabia today*. New York: St. Martin's Press, Inc.

Bain, L.L., & Wendt, J.C. (1983). *Transition to teaching: A guide for the beginning teacher*. Reston, VA: American Alliance for Health, Physical Education, Recreation and Dance.

Banks, J.A. (1997). Multicultural education: Characteristics and goals. In J.A. Banks & C.A.M. Banks (Eds.), *Multicultural education: Issues and perspectives* (3rd ed.) (pp. 3-31). Boston, MA: Allyn and Bacon.

Baruth, L.G., & Manning, M.L. (1992). *Multicultural education of children and adolescents*. Needham Heights, MA: Allyn and Bacon.

Baruth, L.G., & Manning, M.L. (2009). *Multicultural education of children and adolescents* (5th ed.). New York: Pearson.

Blair, T.R. (2003). *New teacher's performance based guide to culturally diverse classrooms*. New York: Pearson Education, Inc.

Blankenship, B.T., & Coleman, M.M. (2009). An examination of "wash-out" and workplace conditions of beginning physical education teachers. *Physical Educator, 66*(2), 97-111.

Blinde, E.M., & McCallister, S.G. (1998). Listening to the voices of students with physical disabilities. *Journal of Physical Education, Recreation and Dance, 69*, 64-68.

Bontempo, D.E., & D'Augelli, A.R. (2002). Effects of at-risk school victimization and sexual orientation on lesbian, gay, or bisexual youth's health risk behaviors. *Journal of Adolescent Health, 30*, 364-374.

Boreen, J., Johnson, M.K., Niday, D., & Potts, J. (2009). *Mentoring beginning teachers: Guiding, reflecting, coaching* (2nd ed.). Portland, ME: Stenhouse Publishers.

Bouchard, C. (1999). Heredity and health-related fitness. In C.B. Corbin & R.P. Pangrazi (Eds.), *Toward a better understanding of physical fitness and activity* (pp. 11-17). Scottsdale, AZ: Holcomb Hathaway Publishers.

Brophy, J., & Good, T. (1986). Teacher behavior and student achievement. In M.C. Wittrock (Ed.), *Handbook of research on teaching* (pp. 328-375). New York: American Educational Research Association.

Brophy, J., & Kher, N. (1986). Teacher socialization as a mechanism for developing student motivation to learn. In R. Feldman (Ed.), *Social psychology applied to education* (pp. 257-288). Cambridge: Cambridge University Press.

Buck, M.M., Lund, J.L., Harrison, J.M., & Cook, C.L. (2007). *Instructional strategies for secondary school physical education* (6th ed.). New York: McGraw-Hill.

Burke, P.J., & McDonnell, J.H. (1992). Competency building. In R. Fessler & J.C. Christensen (Eds.), *The teacher career cycle: Understanding and guiding the professional development of teachers* (pp. 87-118). Boston: Allyn and Bacon.

Cohen, S.A. (1987). Instructional alignment: Searching for the magic bullet. *Educational Researcher, 16*(8), 16-20.

Collier, D.H. (2005). Instructional strategies for adapted physical education. In J.P. Winnick (Ed.), *Adapted physical education and sport* (4th ed.) (pp. 109-130). Champaign, IL: Human Kinetics.

Cone, T.P., & Cone, S.L. (2005). *Teaching children dance* (2nd ed.). Champaign, IL: Human Kinetics.

Corbin, C.B. (2002). Physical activity for everyone: What every physical educator should know about promoting lifelong physical activity. *Journal of Teaching in Physical Education, 21,* 128-144.

Cothran, D.J., & Ennis, C.D. (2001). "Nobody said anything about learning stuff": Students, teachers and curricular change. *Journal of Classroom Interaction, 36*(1), 1-5.

Culp, B.O. (2009). Principles and practices of culturally responsive pedagogy: A brief guide to meeting the needs of ethnically diverse learners in health and physical activity. Retrieved August 8, 2010, from www.culturenmotion.org.

Davis, B.M. (2007). *How to teach students who don't look like you: Culturally relevant teaching strategies.* Thousand Oaks, CA: Corwin Press.

Delpit, L. (1995). *Other people's children: Cultural conflict in the classroom.* New York: New Press.

Diliberto, D. (2009). Who are we? Arabs in America. *Teacher Librarian, 36*(3), 33-34.

Doyle, J.A., & Paludi, M.A. (1998). *Sex and gender: The human experience* (4th ed.). New York: McGraw-Hill.

Dunbar, R.R., & O'Sullivan, M.M. (1986). Effects of intervention on differential treatment of boys and girls in elementary physical education lessons. *Journal of Teaching in Physical Education, 5,* 166-175.

DuRant, R.H., Krowchuk, D.P., & Senal, S.H. (1998). Victimization, use of violence, and drug use at school among lesbian, gay, and bisexual youths. *Journal of Pediatrics, 133,* 113-118.

Elia, J.S. (1986). *An alignment experiment in vocabulary instruction: Varying instructional practice and test item formats to measure transfer with low SES fourth graders.* Doctoral Dissertation, University of San Francisco. Dissertation Abstracts, 48/01A.

Fahey, P.A. (1986). *Learning transfer in main ideas instruction: Effects of instructional alignment and aptitude on main idea test scores.* Doctoral Dissertation, University of San Francisco. Dissertation Abstracts International, 48/03A.

Feghali, E. (1997). Arab cultural communication patterns. *International Journal Intercultural Relations, 21*(3), 345-378.

Fink, J., & Siedentop, D. (1989). The development of routines, rules and expectations at the start of the school year. *Journal of Teaching in Physical Education, 8,* 198-212.

Fuller, M.L. (2001). Multicultural concerns and classroom management. In C.A. Grant & M.L. Gomez (Eds.), *Campus and classroom: Making schooling multicultural* (3rd ed.) (pp. 109-134). Englewood Cliffs, NJ: Prentice Hall.

Graham, G., Holt/Hale, S.A., & Parker, M. (2010). *Children moving: A reflective approach to teaching physical education* (8th ed.). New York: McGraw-Hill.

Griffin, P. (1985). Teachers' perceptions of and responses to sex equity problems in a middle school physical education program. *Research Quarterly for Exercise and Sport, 56,* 103-110.

Hill, G.M., & Cleven, B. (Dec. 2005/Jan. 2006). A comparison of students' choices of 9th grade physical education activities by ethnicity. *The High School Journal, 89*(2), 16-23.

Hodge, S.R., Ammah, J.O.A., Casebolt, K., LaMaster, K., & O'Sullivan, M. (2004). High school general physical education teacher's behavior and beliefs associated with inclusion. *Sport, Education and Society, 9,* 395-419.

Hutzler, Y., Fliess, O., Chacham, A., & van den Auweele, Y. (2002). Perspectives of children with physical disabilities on inclusion and empowerment: Supporting and limiting factors. *Adapted Physical Activity Quarterly, 19,* 300-317.

Joseph, R. (2000). *Stress free teaching: A practical guide to tackling stress in teaching, lecturing and tutoring.* London: Kogan Page Limited.

Katz, L.G. (1972). Developmental stages of preschool teachers. *Elementary School Journal, 73*(1), 50-54.

Koczor, M.L. (1984). *Effects of varying degrees on instructional alignment in posttreatment tests on mastery-learning tasks of fourth-grade children.* Doctoral Dissertation, University of San Francisco. Dissertation Abstracts International, 46/05A.

Kosciw, J.G., Diaz, E.M., & Greytak, E.A. (2008). *2007 national school climate survey: The experiences of lesbian, gay, bisexual and transgender youth in our nation's schools.* New York: GLSEN. Retrieved August 18, 2010, from www.glsen.org.

Lawson, H.A. (1989). From rookie to veteran: Workplace conditions in PE and induction into the profession. In T. Templin & P. Schempp (Eds.), *Socialization into physical education: Learning to teach* (pp. 145-164). Indianapolis: Benchmark Press.

Letven, E. (1992). Induction. In R. Fessler & J.C. Christensen (Eds.), *The teacher career cycle: Understanding and guiding the professional development of teachers* (pp. 59-86). Boston: Allyn and Bacon.

Lieberman, L.J. (Ed.). (2007). *Paraeducators in physical education: A training guide to roles and responsibilities.* Champaign, IL: Human Kinetics.

Lieberman, L.J., & Houston-Wilson, C. (2002). *Strategies for inclusion: A handbook for physical educators.* Champaign, IL: Human Kinetics.

Lieberman, L.J., Houston-Wilson, C., & Kozub, F.M. (2002). Perceived barriers to including students with visual impairments in general physical education. *Adapted Physical Activity Quarterly, 19,* 364-377.

Lindsey, R.B., Robins, K.N., & Terrell, R.D. (2003). *Cultural proficiency: A manual for school leaders.* Thousand Oaks, CA: Corwin Press, Inc.

Lund, J.L., & Kirk, M.F. (2002). *Performance-based assessment for middle and high school physical education.* Champaign, IL: Human Kinetics.

Lund, J.L., & Kirk, M.F. (2010). *Performance-based assessment for middle and high school physical education* (2nd ed.). Champaign, IL: Human Kinetics.

Lund, J., & Tannehill, D. (2010). *Standards-based physical education curriculum development* (2nd ed.). Sudbury, MA: Jones and Bartlett Publishers.

Macdonald, D. (1990). The relationship between sex composition of physical education classes and teacher/pupil verbal interaction. *Journal of Teaching in Physical Education, 9,* 152-163.

Miller, D.K. (2006). *Measurement by the physical educator: Why and how* (5th ed.). New York: McGraw-Hill.

Mitchell, S.A., Oslin, J.L., & Griffin, L.L. (2006). *Teaching sport concepts and skills: A tactical games approach* (2nd ed.). Champaign, IL: Human Kinetics.

Ntoumanis, N. (2001). A self determination approach to the understanding of motivation in physical education. *British Journal of Educational Psychology, 71,* 225-242.

Ntoumanis, N. (2005). A prospective study of participation in optional school physical education using a self-determination theory framework. *Journal of Educational Psychology, 97,* 444-453.

Ntoumanis, N., Pensgaard, A.M., Martin, C., & Pipe, K. (2004). An idiographic analysis of amotivation in compulsory school physical education. *Journal of Sport and Exercise Psychology, 26,* 197-214.

Nydell, M.K. (1996). *Understanding Arabs: A guide for Westerners* (Rev. ed.). Yarmouth, ME: Intercultural Press Inc.

O'Sullivan, M., & Dyson, B. (1994). Rules, routines, and expectations of 11 high school physical education teachers. *Journal of Teaching in Physical Education, 13,* 361-374.

Pangrazi, R.P., & Corbin, C.B. (1990). Age as a factor relating to physical fitness test performance. *Research Quarterly for Exercise and Sport, 61*(4), 410-414.

Pew Forum on Religion and Public Life. (2011). *Muslim Americans: No signs of growth in alienation or support for extremism: Mainstream and moderate attitudes.* Retrieved December 18, 2011, from www.pewforum.org/Muslim/Muslim-Americans--No-Signs-of-Growth-in-Alienation-or-Support-for-Extremism.aspx.

Renn, K.A. (2004). *Mixed race students in college: The ecology of race, identity, and community on campus.* Albany, NY: State University of New York Press.

Rink, J.E. (2010). *Teaching physical education for learning* (6th ed.). New York: McGraw-Hill.

Ryan, R.M., & Deci, E.L. (2000). Self-determination theory and the facilitation of intrinsic motivation, social development, and well being. *American Psychologist, 55,* 68-78.

Schuman, D. (2004). *American schools, American teachers: Issues and perspectives.* New York: Pearson.

Shade, B.J., Kelly, C., & Oberg, M. (1997). *Creating culturally responsive classrooms.* Washington, DC: American Psychological Association.

Siedentop, D., Hastie, P.A., & van der Mars, H. (2011). *Complete guide to sport education* (2nd ed.). Champaign, IL: Human Kinetics.

Siedentop, D., & Tannehill, D. (2000). *Developing teaching skills in physical education* (4th ed.). Mountain View, CA: Mayfield Publishing Company.

Sinagatullin, I.M. (2003). *Constructing multicultural education in a diverse society.* Lanham, MD: The Scarecrow Press, Inc.

Stroot, S.A., & Whipple, C.E. (2003). Organizational socialization: Factors affecting beginning teachers. In S.J. Silverman & C.D. Ennis (Eds.), *Student learning in PE: Applying research to enhance instruction* (2nd ed.) (pp. 311-328). Champaign, IL: Human Kinetics.

Suleiman, M. (2000). *Teaching about Arab Americans: What social studies teachers should know.* Paper presented at the Annual Meeting of the National Social Science Association. Las Vegas, NV, March 26-28, 2000. (ERIC Document Reproduction Service No. ED 442 714)

Tannehill, D., & Zakrajsek, D. (1993). Student attitudes towards physical education: A multicultural study. *Journal of Teaching in Physical Education, 13,* 78-84.

Van Maanen, J., & Schein, E. (1979). Toward a theory of organizational socialization. In B. Staw (Ed.), *Research in organizational behavior* (Vol. 1) (pp. 209-261). Greenwich, CT: JAI Press.

Zeichner, K.E., & Tabachnik, N.R. (1981). Are the effects of university teacher education "washed out" by school practice? *Journal of Teacher Education,32*(3), 7-11.

Index

Note: The italicized *f* and *t* following page numbers refer to figures and tables, respectively.

About the Author

Alisa R. James, EdD, is an associate professor at the College at Brockport, State University of New York. Before entering higher education, James spent eight years teaching elementary and high school physical education. She has been working in physical education teacher education since 2002.

James is a member of the American Alliance for Health, Physical Education, Recreation and Dance (AAHPERD); the National Association for Sport and Physical Education (NASPE) Research Consortium; and New York State Association for Health, Physical Education, Recreation, and Dance (NYSAHPERD). She also served on the executive council of NYSAHPERD for seven years. In 2011, James received the Chancellor's Award for Excellence in Teaching and was nominated for the U.S. Professor of the Year Award at the College of Brockport. She was also named Professional of the Year by NYSAHPERD in 2011.

In her free time, James enjoys playing racquetball, camping, and reading. She lives in Brockport, New York.